Measuring the Statutory and Regulatory Constraints on Department of Defense Acquisition

An Empirical Analysis

Jeffrey A. Drezner, Irv Blickstein, Raj Raman, Megan McKernan,
Monica Hertzman, Melissa A. Bradley, Dikla Gavrieli, Brent Eastwood

Prepared for the Office of the Secretary of Defense
Approved for public release; distribution unlimited

NATIONAL DEFENSE RESEARCH INSTITUTE

The research described in this report was prepared for the Office of the Secretary of Defense (OSD). The research was conducted in the RAND National Defense Research Institute, a federally funded research and development center sponsored by the OSD, the Joint Staff, the Unified Combatant Commands, the Department of the Navy, the Marine Corps, the defense agencies, and the defense Intelligence Community under Contract W74V8H-06-C-0002.

Library of Congress Cataloging-in-Publication Data

Measuring the statutory and regulatory constraints on Department of Defense
  acquisition : an empirical analysis / Jeffrey A. Drezner ... [et al.].
      p. cm.
   Includes bibliographical references.
   ISBN 978-0-8330-4176-0 (pbk. : alk. paper)
      1. United States. Dept. of Defense—Procurement—Evaluation. 2. United States.
  Dept. of Defense—Rules and practice. I. Drezner, Jeffrey A. II. United States. Dept.
  of Defense. III. Title: Measuring the statutory and regulatory constraints on DoD
  acquisition, an empirical analysis.

   UC263.M419 2006
   355.6'2120973—dc22
                                                                        2007030594

The RAND Corporation is a nonprofit research organization providing objective analysis and effective solutions that address the challenges facing the public and private sectors around the world. RAND's publications do not necessarily reflect the opinions of its research clients and sponsors.

RAND® is a registered trademark.

Published 2007 by the RAND Corporation
1776 Main Street, P.O. Box 2138, Santa Monica, CA 90407-2138
1200 South Hayes Street, Arlington, VA 22202-5050
4570 Fifth Avenue, Suite 600, Pittsburgh, PA 15213-2665
RAND URL: http://www.rand.org/
To order RAND documents or to obtain additional information, contact
Distribution Services: Telephone: (310) 451-7002;
Fax: (310) 451-6915; Email: order@rand.org

Preface

Over the past two decades, the Department of Defense (DoD) has been striving to make acquisition-related statutes and regulations less burdensome to program offices. Many studies have focused on the costs of doing business with DoD, but few have attempted to quantify the actual cost of compliance.

The Office of the Under Secretary of Defense for Acquisition, Technology, and Logistics (OUSD/AT&L) requested RAND National Defense Research Institute (NDRI) to quantify the impact of statutes and regulations that are burdensome to program offices. RAND approached this overall research project by (1) identifying which statutes and regulations are perceived as burdensome, (2) developing and validating a methodology to quantify that burden, (3) collecting quantifiable information from program offices, and (4) suggesting relief measures to alleviate the burdensome tasks where possible. This report presents the results of this research. Details of the methodology are discussed in a separate report.[1]

This report should be of interest to program offices, program executive offices within the Military Services, the Office of the Secretary of Defense (OSD), Congress, and contractors with an interest in acquisition policy, processes, and reform.

This research was sponsored by the Office of the Under Secretary of Defense for Acquisition, Technology, and Logistics (OUSD/AT&L) and conducted within the Acquisition and Technology Policy Center of the RAND National Defense Research Institute, a federally funded research and development center sponsored by the Office of the Secretary of Defense, the Joint Staff, the Unified Combatant Commands, the Department of the Navy, the Marine Corps, the defense agencies, and the defense Intelligence Community.

For more information on RAND's Acquisition and Technology Policy Center, contact the Director, Philip Antón. He can be reached by email at atpc-director@rand.org; by phone at 310-393-0411, extension 7798; or by mail at the RAND Corporation, 1776 Main Street, Santa Monica, California 90407-2138. More information about RAND is available at www.rand.org.

---

[1] Drezner et al., 2006.

Contents

Preface iii
Figures vii
Tables ix
Summary xi
Acknowledgments xv
Abbreviations xvii

CHAPTER ONE
Introduction 1
Background and Objectives 1
The Hypothesis 3
Report Organization 4

CHAPTER TWO
Methodology Revisited 7
Overview and Processes 8
Program Selection and Descriptions 8
Data Collection 10
Data Cleaning and Coding 13
Caveats 15

CHAPTER THREE
Results by Statutory and Regulatory Area 17
Aggregate Results 17
Clinger-Cohen Act and Information Management 21
Core Law and 50-50 Rule 23
Program Planning and Budgeting 25
Program Status Reporting 28
Testing 30
Other 33
Sensitivity Analysis 34

CHAPTER FOUR

Special Interest Results 37
An Individual's Time 37
Senior and Nonsenior Participants 39
For Whom Was the Activity Performed? 43
Discrete Events and Processes 44
    DAB-level Interim Program Review Activity 48
    Restructuring a Major Modification Program 51

CHAPTER FIVE

Conclusions 55
Comparison with Similar Research 57
Policy Implications and Recommendations 59
Suggested Areas for Future Research 61

APPENDIX A

Program Data by Statutory and Regulatory Area 63

Bibliography 79

Figures

1.1   The Hypothesis Being Tested 3
3.1   Compliance Level of Effort as a Percentage of Total Available Hours 18
3.2   Distribution of Time Spent Across Regulatory Areas (1) 18
3.3   Distribution of Time Spent Across Regulatory Areas (2) 19
3.4   Program Office Effort in the CCA Regulatory Area 21
3.5   Program Office Effort in the Core Law and 50-50 Rule Regulatory Area 24
3.6   Program Office Effort in the PPB Regulatory Area 26
3.7   Level of Effort for What-if Exercises 27
3.8   Program Office Effort in the PSR Regulatory Area 29
3.9   Level of Effort for PSR "Other" 30
3.10 Program Office Effort in the Testing Regulatory Area 31
3.11 Program Office Effort in the "Other" Regulatory Area 33
4.1   Proportion of Time Spent on Compliance Activities
      by Each Study Participant (1) 38
4.2   Proportion of Time Spent on Compliance Activities
      by Each Study Participant (2) 39
4.3   Total Senior-Level and Nonsenior-Level Hours by Regulatory Area
      Across All Seven Programs 41
4.4   Senior-Level versus Nonsenior-Level Cumulative Person-Equivalents
      by Program 42
4.5   DAB IPR Activity, Program A 51
4.6   Restructuring a Major Modification, Program G 54
5.1   Debunking the Myth 56

Tables

2.1   Summary Participation at Each Program Office......................12
3.1   Annual Level of Effort for CCA Compliance by Program 22
3.2   Annual Level or Effort for Core/50-50 Compliance by Program................24
3.3   Annual Level of Effort for PPB Compliance by Program......................27
3.4   Annual Level of Effort for PSR Compliance by Program......................29
3.5   Annual Level of Effort for Test Compliance by Program.....................32
3.6   Sensitivity Analysis of Top-Level Results...............................35
4.1   Average Hours per Nonsenior and Senior-Level Worker by Regulatory Area....41
4.2   Average Hours per Nonsenior and Senior-Level Worker by Program............43
4.3   For Whom Was the Compliance Activity Performed?......................45
4.4   Selected Activities Associated with Selected Events and Processes................46
4.5   Preparation Activities for DAB IPR, Program A......................50
4.6   Restructuring a Major Modification, Program G 53
A.1   User Information and Hours for Program A (By Reporting Period) 64
A.2   User Information and Hours for Program B (By Reporting Period) 66
A.3   User Information and Hours for Program C (By Reporting Period) 68
A.4   User Information and Hours for Program D (By Reporting Period)...............70
A.5   User Information and Hours for Program E (By Reporting Period) 72
A.6   User Information and Hours for Program F (By Reporting Period) 74
A.7   User Information and Hours for Program G (By Reporting Period)..............76

Summary

Improving the defense acquisition process has been a recurring theme for several decades. Acquisition process reforms often require changes in the body of statutes and regulations governing the acquisition process. Prior research has observed a "regulatory pendulum" in which statutes and regulations seem to move back and forth from relative flexibility to relative rigidity in response to perceived problems in the acquisition process generally, or in specific weapon system programs. Increased flexibility enables program managers to tailor their program's acquisition strategy to the unique features of its environment and to reduce the costs of oversight. Rigidity in statutes and regulations mandates specific management approaches and oversight procedures. Program managers often complain that the periods of relative rigidity constrain their ability to manage their program effectively and impose real, non-value-added costs on the program.

This research addresses the perceived problem of overly burdensome statutes and regulations directly. The objective of this research was to quantify and document the effects of a specific statute or regulation on a specific weapon system program. While many other studies have addressed this topic, few have succeeded in generating the empirical evidence needed to inform the policy debate with more than just anecdotes.

This research tests the hypothesis that the statutes and regulations governing defense acquisition programs place constraints on those programs that significantly affect the program manager's ability to manage the program. There is a widespread perception in the acquisition community that significant portions of program office staff spend an inordinate amount of time responding to statutes and regulations through formal compliance activities and informal processes that have developed around those activities. Much of that compliance-related time is perceived as burdensome, with purported consequences of schedule delays, additional incurred costs, loss of weapon system capability, increased demands on critical program staff, and other impacts on program execution and outcomes.

As described in our Phase 1 report,[1] we developed a Web-based data collection tool that enabled participants to input the time spent on specific compliance-related activities and provide comments related to those activities. The data collection tool

---

[1] Drezner et al., 2006.

listed all the compliance activities we had identified in each of five regulatory areas: Clinger-Cohen Act, Core Law and 50-50 Rule, program planning and budgeting, program status reporting, and testing. The tool provided space to report other compliance activities in each area as well as other statutory or regulatory areas of interest to individual participants. We recruited seven program offices as participants and asked that they identify all program office and associated personnel who perform activities relevant to those five areas. We asked those identified individuals to enter data (hours worked on specific activities and any associated comments) every two weeks for a 12-month period. We assembled interim results for each program and reviewed those results with each program every two to three months to validate the information provided. Overall, 316 individuals in the seven program offices participated during the study field period. These individuals included program managers, deputy program managers, product managers, and branch chiefs, as well as personnel within the functional areas associated with the five statutory and regulatory areas of interest.

The results were rather surprising:

- The total reported time spent on compliance activities in the five statutory and regulatory areas we addressed was less than 5 percent of the total staff time available to each program office.
- Most program office officials do not work full time on compliance activities in these five areas. In fact, the vast majority of participants reported considerably less than 20 percent of their total work time as relating to compliance activities in the five areas studied.
- Most compliance-related activities are performed in reference to a Service request or requirement, rather than OSD, Government Accounting Office (GAO), or other program stakeholders.
- In discussions and in their comments input to the Web-based data protocol, participants emphasized process-related issues (i.e., implementation—the details of how compliance is achieved) rather than the intent of a statute or regulation. Participants recognized that many of these "compliance" activities need to be accomplished regardless of whether they are mandated.
- Few serious complaints were recorded about policies or processes within these five statutory or regulatory areas, and reported hours are not correlated with complaints. That is, the majority of complaints reflect the participant's view that the activity was burdensome, even if it took little time to accomplish. The explanation appears to be that deviations from an individual's perceived normal job functions are often perceived as burdensome.
- There is little evidence of actual consequences to program execution or outcomes as a result of the compliance activities we tracked. We could identify only a single example in which a firm link could be established between a statute and its associated regulatory processes and program cost and schedule outcomes.

Programs are indeed governed by a large and confusing array of statutes and regulations, and those statutes and regulations do place constraints on program execution. But program office staff do not appear to spend a significant amount of their time complying with those statutes and regulations, nor is much of that compliance time perceived as burdensome. Lastly, there are few adverse consequences to program outcomes due to compliance activities associated with the statutes and regulations we studied.

These findings do not mean that regulatory compliance is without costs, and some compliance activities may indeed be non-value added or burdensome. Many program office personnel who have not formally tracked time spent on such activities certainly perceive that they spend a significant amount of time complying with statutes and regulations perceived as non-value added or burdensome; however, no evidence supports this perception. It was notable that our study participants began with this view, but ended the study agreeing that perhaps the difference between perception and reality was significant.

We made several observations over the course of the study that suggest ways to mitigate some of the perceived burden that was reported:

- Both the perceived burden and reported time spent in compliance activities were driven largely by the unique characteristics of the program and the challenges and issues it is currently facing. This argues for a high degree of flexibility and tailoring of compliance activities, balanced by clear implementation guidance and sufficient training for program office personnel.
- For some compliance activities, technical support to program offices—provided by functional offices within the Service acquisition staff or commodity command—would improve the effectiveness of implementation as well as reduce perceived burdens.
- The introduction of a new policy or procedure will cause a spike in program office compliance activity. If program offices are provided clearer guidance and technical support, the length and severity of the compliance spike can be reduced.

We could not identify any areas in which policy change or streamlined implementation would save significant dollars in program management funds or reduce program cycle times. Nor could we identify a set of program office personnel who do nothing but comply with non-value-added or burdensome statutes and regulations, and whose jobs would not be necessary if changes in statutes and regulations and implementing processes were made. The belief that these kinds of savings would result from reform is part of the myth that motivated this research; we found little data in direct support of that hypothesis and considerable evidence refuting it.

The very idea of value-added versus non-value-added compliance activities raises an important question: Value to whom? What values are these activities designed to add? While some compliance costs may accrue to organizations that perceive such activities as valueless, such as program offices, other organizations or the Department of Defense (DoD) enterprise as a whole may obtain significant value (benefit) from those same activities. Exploring the benefit side of the equation (i.e., who gets what kind of benefit from activities related to statutory and regulatory compliance?) may provide additional insight to policy makers in the acquisition community as they weigh the advantages and disadvantages of acquisition process streamlining initiatives.

Acknowledgments

We extend our gratitude and appreciation to all the program office staff, Service personnel, and Office of the Secretary of Defense and industry officials who gave their time and insights in support of this research.

Special thanks are due to the program managers and staff of the seven programs that participated in the field portion of the study reported here. Their continuous participation over a 12-month period and their willingness to provide information on the what, why, and how of compliance activities were exceptional. This research would not have been possible without their cooperation in providing the information we asked for and their comments and suggestions on how to interpret that information in proper context. We greatly appreciate the efforts of all our study participants.

Our colleagues Giles Smith and Kathi Webb provided excellent technical reviews of the draft report. Their comments and suggestions greatly improved the final product. We also gratefully acknowledge the outstanding administrative support provided by Maria Falvo throughout the research and writing phases.

Any errors are the responsibility of the authors.

Abbreviations

ACAT	Acquisition Category
AoA	Analysis of Alternatives
APB	Acquisition Program Baseline
ASN RDA	Assistant Secretary of the Navy for Research, Acquisition, and Development
ASR	Acquisition Strategy Report
AT&L	Acquisition, Technology, and Logistics
C4ISP	Command, Control, Communication, Computers, and Intelligence Support Plan
CAIG	Cost Analysis Improvement Group
CARD	Cost Analysis Requirements Document
CCA	Clinger-Cohen Act
CCDR	Contractor Cost Data Report
CIO	Chief Information Officer
CPAR	Contractor Performance Assessment
DAB	Defense Acquisition Board
DAB IPR	Defense Acquisition Board Interim Program Review
DAES	Defense Acquisition Executive Summary
DFAR	Defense Federal Acquisition Regulations
DoD	Department of Defense
DOT&E	Director, Operational Test and Evaluation

EAC	Estimate at Completion
EVM	Earned value management
EVSMA	Enterprise Value Stream Mapping Assessment
FAR	Federal Acquisition Regulations
FRP	Full Rate Production
FTE	Full-time equivalent
GAO	Government Accounting Office
GIG	Global Information Grid
GWOT	Global war on terror
IA	Information Assurance
IIPT	Interim Integrated Product Team
IMS	Integrated Master Schedule
IPR	Interim Program Review
ISP	Information Support Plan
IT	Information technology
ITAB	Information Technology Acquisition Board
JSOW	Joint stand-off weapon
JTA	Joint Technical Architecture
LCCE	Life-cycle cost estimate
LRIP	Low Rate Initial Production
LRIP/IOT&E	LRIP/Initial Operational Test and Evaluation
MDAPS	Major defense acquisitions programs
NAVSEA	Naval Sea Systems Command
NDRI	National Defense Research Institute
O&M	Operations and Maintenance
OIPT	Overarching Integrated Product Team
ORD	Operational Requirements Document

OSD	Office of the Secretary of Defense
OTRR	Operational Test Readiness Review
OUSD	Office of the Under Secretary of Defense
PEO	Program Executive Officer
PM	Program Manager
POC	Point of contact
POE	Program office estimate
PPB	Program planning and budget
PSR	Program status reporting
RDT&E	Research, Development, Test, and Evaluation
RTOC	Reduction in total ownership cost
SAF/AQ	Secretary of the Air Force/Acquisition
SAMP	Single Acquisition Management Plan
SAR	Selected Acquisition Report
SEP	System Engineering Plan
TDY	Temporary Duty
TEMP	Test and Evaluation Master Pan
UCR	Unit Cost Report
UID	Unique identification
WIPT	Working Integrated Product Team

CHAPTER ONE

Introduction

Improving the defense acquisition process has been a continuous goal of both Congress and the Department of Defense (DoD) for several decades. Most acquisition reform initiatives have focused on improving the cost, schedule, and performance outcomes of major defense acquisition programs (MDAPs). These reforms often require changes in the body of statutes and regulations governing the acquisition process. Prior research has observed a "regulatory pendulum" in which statutes and regulations seem to move from relative flexibility to relative rigidity in response to perceived problems in the acquisition process generally, or in specific weapon system programs. Flexibility enables program managers to tailor their program's acquisition strategy to the unique features of its environment and to reduce the costs of oversight. Rigidity in statutes and regulations can be thought of as the opposite extreme—mandating specific management approaches and oversight procedures. Program managers often complain that the periods of relative rigidity constrain their ability to manage their program effectively, and that they impose real, non-value-added costs to the program. This research directly addresses this issue.

Background and Objectives

The perception that a significant regulatory burden is placed on DoD acquisition programs is widespread. Every program office official has at least one anecdote about how time-consuming and costly compliance with a particular statute or regulation is (or was). However, officials are rarely able to provide an estimate of compliance cost or any other quantitative impact on the program (e.g., schedule delay while waiting for approval of a document). Recently, several attempts were made to quantify such costs:[1]

- The joint stand-off weapon (JSOW) program estimated a cost to the program office of $3.4 million in government and contractor support labor hours (21,918 hours) to prepare and obtain approval for documents required in support of its

---

[1] These efforts are described in more detail, and their results are compared with ours, later in this report.

Milestone C low-rate production decision. The program estimates that a significant amount of such costs are non-value added to the program.[2]

- Similarly, the Navy's Program Executive Officer (PEO) Carriers office estimated that preparation of Milestone B documentation for the CVN-21 program took 245,804 hours of direct labor over a three- to four-year period, and included people in the CVN-21 program office, PEO Carriers, Naval Sea Systems Command (NAVSEA) supporting organizations, and contractors.[3]
- The Air Force conducted a review of the oversight processes associated with its MDAPs in which program managers identified several Office of the Secretary of Defense (OSD)-oriented meetings as particularly burdensome (e.g., Working Integrated Product Team [WIPT], Interim Integrated Product Team [IIPT], and Overarching Integrated Product Team [OIPT]) meetings leading to a Defense Acquisition Board [DAB]-level decision).[4]

These examples appear to lend empirical support to the constant stream of anecdotes from program offices about how time-consuming, costly, and burdensome certain statutory and regulatory compliance activities are. Senior OSD and Service acquisition officials have taken these anecdotes and evidence seriously, continuing the search for ways to make the acquisition process less burdensome at the program office level while maintaining the level of oversight and accountability required in the expenditure of public funds.

The objective of the present research was to quantify and document the effects of a specific statute or regulation on a specific weapon system program. While many other studies have addressed this topic, few have succeeded in generating the empirical evidence needed to raise the policy debate above the level of anecdotes. Thus, part of our objective was to design and test a methodology that can be used to generate such empirical data.

To accomplish this objective, we designed a study that addressed the following research questions:

- What statutes and regulations are perceived as burdensome at the program office level?
- What are the specific compliance activities associated with these statutes and regulations?
- How can the impact of those activities be measured?
- What are the impacts of compliance activities at the program level?
- How can adverse impacts be mitigated?

---

[2] Young, July 22, 2005.

[3] Data file (Man Hours MS B Documents 4-08-04) provided to RAND by PEO Carriers.

[4] Graham, June 21, 2005.

A separately published report addresses the first three questions; it describes in detail our research approach, the process we used to identify statutes and regulations perceived as burdensome, and the Web-based data collection protocol and associated analytical procedures we used.[5] This report presents the final results of the research. It also updates the methods we used and describes how they worked in practice.

The Hypothesis

This research tests a specific hypothesis, illustrated in Figure 1.1, that has been treated as conventional wisdom within the acquisition community. Simply stated, the hypothesis is that the statutes and regulations governing defense acquisition programs place constraints on those programs that significantly affect the program manager's ability to manage the program. Program office staff spend an inordinate amount of time responding to those statutes and regulations through formal compliance activities and informal processes that have developed around those activities. Much of that compliance-related time, whether formal or informal, is perceived as burdensome from the program's perspective and is perceived to have real consequences on program execution and outcomes. These adverse effects or consequences of regulatory compliance include schedule delays, additional costs incurred, loss of weapon system capability, increased demands on critical program staff, or other impacts on program execution and outcomes.

Figure 1.1
The Hypothesis Being Tested

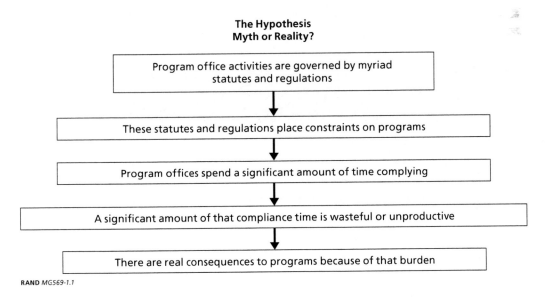

RAND *MG569-1.1*

---

5 Drezner et al., 2006.

Based on numerous anecdotes associated with this cause-and-effect assertion, the acquisition community appears to believe that significant time is spent complying with non-value-added statutory and regulatory requirements, resulting in significant consequences for the programs. Most often those consequences are expressed as time lost waiting for the necessary approvals or "working the system" to make those approvals happen, added costs to the program in terms of direct labor hours and travel time (e.g., to Washington to brief Pentagon officials), as well as the diversion of attention of senior program office staff from the more important job of managing the program. Quantitatively, the anecdotes we have heard over several decades lead us to an expectation that about half the people in a program office spend most of their time on compliance activities, most of which is viewed as non-value added at the program level. During periods in which the program office is preparing for a major program review or milestone decision, those numbers might increase. If correct, this situation represents a significant level of effort going toward activities of limited usefulness to the program.

Despite the wide acceptance of this hypothesis, there is little or no empirical evidence that it is in fact true. It is the absence of such evidence that this study is attempting to address.

As stated, the hypothesis adopts a program office perspective in the sense that activities not directly relevant to managing the program's progress are perceived as non-value added or burdensome. From a broader perspective, it is important to realize that statutes and regulations are intended to have benefits as well as costs. Benefits include providing mechanisms for oversight and accountability, preserving information on program status and decision making, and formalizing decision processes, among others. In the set of statutes and regulations we addressed in this study, we found that the compliance costs often accrue at the program level while benefits accrue at higher organizational levels in the Military Services, OSD, and Congress. This study has not addressed the benefits question directly, but it is important to acknowledge that statutes and regulations have a purpose that must be identified and weighed in comparison with their compliance costs.

Report Organization

Chapter Two of this report revisits our research approach. In particular, we describe how the data collection process actually worked, and how we cleaned, processed, and analyzed the information obtained. We provide general information on each participating program and describe the participation rates of individuals within each program.

Chapter Three presents research results at the program level for each statutory and regulatory area. We provide detailed results by specific activity within each area. A sensitivity analysis explores how these results change as a function of assumptions about the quality of participation.

Chapter Four presents additional results from several different perspectives. We first describe the results at an individual level by showing how much time an individual in a program office spends on compliance in the five statutory and regulatory areas we examined. We then present selected results that differentiate between senior and non-senior participants. This section presents information on the office (i.e., Congress, OSD, Service, PEO, or the program) for which the participants thought that compliance activities were being performed. Lastly, we discuss the data from the perspective of discrete events or processes that program officials identified as burdensome or otherwise worth tracking.

In Chapter Five, we summarize our results and compare our findings with those of several similar efforts undertaken in approximately the same time frame as our study. We then draw implications from our findings for policy design and implementation, and suggest areas that require further research.

Appendix A contains data tables for each participating program showing the raw data (hours reported) by statutory and regulatory area, as well as by specific activity within those areas.

CHAPTER TWO

Methodology Revisited

As described in our Phase 1 report,[1] interviews conducted with a wide range of acquisition process stakeholders (program managers and staff, PEOs, Service functional staff, OSD functional staff, and congressional research organizations) resulted in the identification of five statutory and regulatory areas to study in Phase 2 of the project:

- Clinger-Cohen Act (CCA), which encompasses management of information technology (IT);
- Core Law and 50-50 Rule (also called Core/50-50), which mandates that at least 50 percent of weapon system maintenance work be performed at and by government organizations;
- Program planning and budgeting (PPB), which encompasses the financial management and resource allocation process;
- Program status reporting (PSR), which includes mandated periodic reporting, ad hoc requests for information, and oversight processes; and
- Testing, which includes activities related to test planning.

Each of these areas is composed of a specific set of compliance activities performed by program office staff. We identified those activities through discussion with program, Service, and OSD officials, as well as a thorough review of applicable statutes, regulations, and implementing directives.

Tracking the actual time spent on compliance activities by program office staff was determined to be the most direct way of quantifying the level of effort at the program office. By collecting these hours over a 12-month period we hoped to capture the ebb and flow of activities over the course of an annual cycle at the program office. Additionally, by conducting follow-up interviews with program office staff on specific comments provided during the data collection period, we hoped to gain a better understanding of how particular compliance tasks are related to program outcomes.

---

[1] Drezner et al., 2006.

Overview and Processes

As described in our Phase 1 report,[2] we developed an easy-to-use Web-based data collection tool that enabled participants to input the time spent on designated activities and provide qualitative comments related to those activities. The data collection tool listed all the compliance activities we identified in each of the five regulatory areas; it provided space to report other compliance activities in each area as well as other statutory or regulatory areas of interest to individual participants. The data collection tool also provided space in which participants could type qualitative comments regarding a particular activity.

We decided that using a two-week data collection period, similar to a two-week timekeeping period, was a good compromise for the research design; it balances the ease for program office staff to remember their activities while not appearing so time-consuming as to discourage participation. The field period—the period of time participants in each program were asked to report on relevant activities—for each of the seven participating programs was 52 weeks divided into 26 two-week study periods. The participating programs began reporting at different times, but all seven reported compliance activities for 26 consecutive two-week periods.

Program Selection and Descriptions

We used fairly simple criteria to select programs for participation. We wanted mainly Acquisition Category (ACAT) I programs, since it is these large and highly visible programs to which much of the governing body of statutes and regulations are directed. We wanted at least one program from each military service to test for differences in compliance activities across services. We wanted at least one program in each of the main weapon system program life-cycle phases—development, production, and supporting fielded systems. Study resources constrained the number of programs we could accommodate to around six. Through our client, we contacted acquisition officials within each of the services and asked them to identify candidate programs for participation in the study. We had contacted officials from some of these programs during our Phase 1 research design activities. Of the eight programs we asked to participate, seven did so for the full study field period.[3]

To encourage participation, we assured each program office that no data would be released that associated a particular data entry or finding with a particular program. We made a similar assurance of confidentiality to individual participants to encourage candid input to the study. Participating programs were shown their own reported data

---

[2] Drezner et al., 2006.

[3] The eighth program was removed from the study by mutual consent. Study participation was purely voluntary, and such participation clearly required significant extra effort by participating individuals.

periodically as part of our validation approach, but individual data inputs were not shared. To maintain this confidentiality, we use letters to identify the seven programs—Programs A through G. Programs were assigned letters in no particular order. In the discussions that follow, we refer to programs using these letters, and if necessary, we refer to individuals within those programs by their functional job title.

The following discussion briefly describes each participating program along several dimensions that are helpful in interpreting the data for a specific program, as well as interpreting the overall results. We cannot provide detailed descriptions because that would violate the assurance of anonymity that we gave each participating program.

Program A is a relatively young program of moderate size; it is still in development and consequently producing hardware at a low rate. It has a high IT component. Approximately 130 personnel work in the program office. The program's acquisition strategy was in flux throughout the study period, largely due to changing requirements. The program reported difficulty in meeting cost and testing goals, with additional risk reported in schedule and performance aspects. The program's Defense Acquisition Executive Summary (DAES) report indicated at least one cost or schedule breach during the field period. Developmental configurations of the system were successfully supporting deployed troops in the global war on terror (GWOT). Given its situation, place in the life cycle, and content, we would expect relatively more reported compliance activity in the PSR, PPB, CCA, and testing categories.

Program B is a relatively young program in development with a high IT component. It was a relatively small program office with approximately 120 personnel. The program's acquisition strategy used an evolutionary approach to development; during the study period, several early configurations were being deployed while improved versions were in various stages of planning and development. Given program content and life cycle, we would expect relatively more activity in CCA and testing.

Program C is a mature program with different configurations simultaneously deployed and operational, in production, and in development. The development activity is centered on a major modification to the basic system, which passed its Milestone B several years before the study period. The program office is relatively small, with about 120 personnel. Given its complexity and content, we would expect Program C to have relatively more activity in PPB and PSR, along with testing activities for the major modification element of the program. While it has a high IT component, the program satisfied the CCA compliance requirements before the study period.

Programs D and E are quite similar, although they are managed in different Services. Both are mature programs nearing the end of their production phase. There are no plans for a major modification in either program, but program office and contractor analyses have been examining such issues. Smaller sets of upgrades have been made throughout the life cycles of both programs. Program D has a relatively small program office of 120 people, while Program E has a large program office with 250 people. Both are ACAT IC programs. Both programs are relatively high-dollar-value programs and thus attracted significant activity in the PPB area. Program D had significant ongoing test activity that included both planning and execution. Program E had few programmatic or technical issues during the course of the study.

Program F is an ACAT II program with many component subprograms. Some of these are in production or deployed with troops supporting GWOT activities, and others are in various stages of development. It is a small program office with about 120 personnel. Program office personnel support other programs, both ACAT I and II, being managed within the same Service. We would expect relatively more activities in testing and PSR, given that many elements of the program were in development during the course of the study.

Program G is a large, mature program; one configuration is in the middle of its production phase, while a major modification is in early development. The program office manages several smaller upgrade projects as well as several operations and support field activities. The program office has about 250 people. With components of the program in different stages of their life cycles, Program G presents a relatively complex management challenge, with activities using all categories of funding. Given its situation, we expected relatively more PPB, PSR, and testing-related compliance activities.

Data Collection

Program managers were asked to identify individuals working in their programs who spend time complying with the specific statutes or regulations of interest for the study. These individuals made up the initial participant groups. Before the start of each program's participation in the study, we made a site visit to brief participants on the purpose of the study and to train them on the use of the Web-based tool.

Participants were provided with a User Manual and a Quick Start Guide for the Web-based tool.[4] Participants who registered at later dates or who were not able to attend the training session were sent electronic copies of these documents. Once training was complete, we asked program staff to register with the study. More details on the registration process are described in our Phase 1 report.

Participants were asked to access the study Web form at least once during each two-week entry period to log hours worked on activities related to specific statutes or regulations. The system allowed the participant to access the form multiple times during an entry period. Within a given period, each time a participant accessed the Web site, prior data entries for that period were shown and could be modified. Participants were required to "close out" each two-week study period by the last Sunday of that period. A study period had to be closed out before data for the next study period

---

[4]   These are published as appendixes in the companion report. See Drezner et al., 2006.

could be entered. Once the period was closed out, the participant could not access or modify the entries from that period.

Program participation began at different times, based on our ability to recruit and train participating personnel. Two programs began data collection on June 28, 2004: one initially enrolling 55 participants and the other enrolling 28 participants. One program began participation on August 23, 2004, with 14 participants; three more programs began reporting on September 6, 2004, with enrollments of 59, 31, and 9 participants. The final program enrolled on October 4, 2004, with 15 participants. The actual number of participants for each program varied throughout their 52-week field periods. Participants who left the program were removed from further participation in the study; additional participants were removed or enrolled at the request of the program manager. A more detailed description of program participation is provided below.

Once data collection began, a variety of follow-up activities were employed to encourage participation. Each two-week study period closed on a Sunday; participants who had not closed out their entries received an email prompt the following Monday (and, if necessary, also one week later) reminding them to do so. If the period had still not been closed out by the second Sunday after the period ended, the project team closed out the participant's account; this type of closeout was designated as an "administrative closeout." When a participant had a long series of "administrative closeouts," RAND project personnel attempted to contact the participant directly, or enlisted the assistance of the program manager or designate to determine whether the participant was still eligible for the study and whether the individual needed further encouragement to participate.

Table 2.1 summarizes the participation at each program office. As mentioned above, program participation varied throughout the field period as program staff were removed or enrolled in the study. The tables in Appendix A show the number of participants in each program for each period over the course of the study. During the course of data collection, a total of 316 program staff enrolled in the study.

After each program had participated for several data collection periods, a follow-up site visit was made to review the study and preliminary findings with the program staff. Based on these meetings and on other contacts with program managers or their designates, adjustments were made to the participant lists; some participants were dropped from the study and others were added. Program B and Program E made significant adjustments to their lists, primarily eliminating participants who did not spend time complying with the specific statutes or regulations of interest for the study. In addition, for a few programs, hours were adjusted or backfilled in coordination with specific participants.

Keeping the participants engaged over a 12-month reporting time frame was a difficult task. In each program, we were assisted by a single point of contact (POC) who was designated by the program manager as the liaison between the participating program office staff and the RAND research team. These POCs encouraged their

Table 2.1
Summary Participation at Each Program Office

	Number of Participants at Start of Data Collection	Number of Participants at End of Data Collection	Number of Program Staff to Ever Participate
Program A	31	31	39
Program B[a]	9	7	19
Program C	28	27	30
Program D	14	39	46
Program E[b]	59	52	86
Program F	15	29	32
Program G	55	50	64

[a] Includes ten participants who were later removed because they did not spend time complying with specific statutes or regulations of interest for the study. Data provided by these participants are not included in the final participation reports or analysis files.

[b] Includes 11 participants who were later removed because they did not spend time complying with specific statutes or regulations of interest for the study. Data provided by these participants are not included in the final participation reports or analysis files.

program office colleagues to keep their participation up to date. In addition to the reminder emails RAND sent out, most POCs sent out their own reminder emails to participants. The POCs also called individual participants if we felt that something was wrong with their participation or input. Most important, several of the program offices discussed the RAND study at their weekly staff meetings. These discussions, while brief, usually included an expression of support from the program manager or deputy, a reminder to log on and provide input, and identification of specific program activities for that week that were relevant to our study. We sent the POCs participation statistics every couple of months so they could verify that the right people were enrolled and that the reporting pattern (whether or not they reported data in a given period) appeared reasonable.

We visited the program offices at least once every three months to show study participants the data they had provided in the preceding quarter. At these visits, we asked study participants to validate their own data; participants were asked if the hours they reported in each time period on specific compliance activities really reflected the time they spent on such activities. In most cases, participants validated the input; in some cases, we adjusted the reported hours to include either additional time spent on a previously reported activity in a specific period, or time spent on a relevant activity that had not been reported and should have been.

At the close of each program's field period, participants were sent an email thanking them for their participation and notifying them that their program had completed the data collection field period. The final program ended its participation on October 2, 2005.

Data Cleaning and Coding

The information each participant recorded on the Web form was captured in a database. The raw data were validated and cleaned as they were transformed into a database suitable for analysis. At the close of each data collection period, a raw data file containing the activities, time spent, and comments entered by each participant for that period was downloaded from the Web-based system. Each line of the data file represents the time a participant spent on a specific activity for a specific time period. Participants could (and generally did) record several lines of data for each period, each individual data line representing time spent on a different activity during the period.

The database file for each period was reviewed for the following items: zero hours (participants indicated they worked zero hours on an activity), reported vacation time, holidays, and other noncompliance activity hours that were reported. These noncompliance activity data lines were annotated in the raw data file and ultimately excluded from the file used in the analysis. Columns were added to the database file to allow calculation of total hours (a combination of the hours and minutes columns that participants recorded) and a seniority code (participants were coded as "senior" or "non-senior" based on their rank or pay grade). The database file for that period was then passed to the project team for coding and inclusion in the master analysis file.

To help analyze the data, project team members reviewed and coded each line of data into five categories useful for the analysis:

- Product area or the specific program element that the compliance activity related to (e.g., main system, product line, or major modification);
- Functional activity or exactly what type of activity was performed (e.g., information development, document review, meeting preparation);
- Report type or the specific document (or process) being referred to, such as Test and Evaluation Master Plan (TEMP), Acquisition Strategy Report (ASR), System Engineering Plan (SEP), Information Assurance (IA) Strategy;
- User task (i.e., exactly what did this particular individual do as part of the compliance activity?); and
- For whom the task was completed (i.e., the perceived source or driver of the compliance activity).

This last category—for whom the task was performed—used a combination of the explanatory comments accompanying the hours for each specific activity reported and the list of "for whom" check boxes in which the participant indicated all the stakeholders for whom a particular task was performed. Not every line could be coded with a category. We drew on user comments, program office discussions, and our knowledge of program content and context to give each line of data one or more codes to support subsequent analysis.

On the final page of the Web-based input form, two general text fields captured additional information that a participant might want to convey about that period. One was a simple text box labeled "general comments," intended for the participant to provide comments on any issue of concern. The second field asked if there was anything else we needed to know about compliance activities in the current period. In addition to the raw data file, at the close of each data collection period, a participant comment file containing the information provided by users in these two text fields was downloaded and reviewed. These comments contained a wide variety of information, including vacation and holiday notices, travel notices, and additional information about the program or tasks for the period. Substantive comments were forwarded to the study team for review.

Program-level "zero-hours reports" were created each reporting period to track participant enrollment and withdrawals from the study. These reports detailed the type of "closeout" for each user in a program and whether the user had entered data during that period. The zero-hours reports also tracked vacation hours reported in the raw data files, participant comments files, and vacation notifications received via email from participants.

The individual participant-level information captured in the zero-hours reports was used to create "program participation reports" for each program in each period. These reports characterized users into three categories: those who provided no data during the field period, those who provided data but never in any of the statutory and regulatory activities of interest (e.g., all "other" data),[5] and those who provided data in the statutory and regulatory activities of interest for at least one study period ("legitimate participants"). These reports detailed enrollment numbers, the universe of possible staff hours, and holiday and vacation hours for each program during each study period. The program participation reports were used by the research team to get a sense of overall participation patterns for each user and the program as a whole. We periodically sent these reports to the program POCs for review and validation, and for identification of additional staff who should be enrolled or withdrawn.

The participation reports for each program were used to calculate the unique "person-equivalent" factor for each program in each period. These factors were used to convert the hours reported on relevant compliance activities into our person-equivalent metric, which is roughly equivalent to a full-time equivalent (FTE) metric.[6] We dis-

---

[5]   The Web forms allowed participants to record time spent against compliance activities not related to the five focus areas of the study. These were grouped in an "other statutes and regulations" category. Several program offices elected to track compliance time against specific activities (e.g., the Uniform Identification Code policy). Data in the "other statutes and regulations" category were handled separately from the data in our five focus areas.

[6]   This metric is very similar to the more familiar full-time equivalent (FTE) measure often used in labor analyses. A person-equivalent is derived from the total available hours registered participants could have spent in each period, accounting for reported vacations, sick leave, and holidays. Each reporting period nominally contained 80 hours of possible work time (assuming no overtime). After subtracting holidays and reported vacation time, the person-equivalent metric was usually less than 80 hours per period for all programs.

covered early in the feedback process that presenting the reported data as "400 hours spent on compliance activities within a particular statutory and regulatory area" was difficult for program office personnel to assess. Is 400 hours a lot or a little? How does it compare with time spent on other activities? If, however, we presented the same data as "the equivalent of five people working full time on these compliance activities over this two-week period," program personnel found it easier to interpret. If you also know that a program office has 100 people working in it, then this number immediately suggests a relative level-of-effort metric referenced to the total number of people in a program office.

A person-equivalent is derived from the total available hours registered participants could have spent in each period, accounting for reported vacations, sick leave, and holidays. An individual working full time in a program office over a two-week period can theoretically work a total of 80 hours.[7] On average, person-equivalent values varied across programs and time periods from the upper 60s to upper 70s after accounting for holidays, sick time, and vacations. For instance, in a two-week period containing a national holiday (e.g., President's Day), the total possible time an individual could work was reduced to 72 hours. If that particular program reported a total of 124 hours in the PPB statutory area, that would be equivalent to 1.72 person-equivalents of effort against PPB compliance. So the equivalent of just under one and three-quarters of an FTE was spent on PPB compliance activities by that program office during that period.

In calculating the total available hours for the program participation reports, participant-reported vacation hours were removed from the total available hours for each period. As noted above, participants reported vacation hours in the raw data files, in participant comments files, and through vacation notifications sent by email to the project alias. Although participants could notify the project of extended travel or Temporary Duty (TDY) using the Web-based form, this form did not specify whether time away was due to vacation. Vacation time was removed from the total available hours for the program participation reports only for participants specifically indicating vacation hours. Therefore, it is likely that these hours are underreported.

Caveats

The success of this approach to quantifying program office costs of compliance rests on several key assumptions:

- Programs would agree to participate,

---

[7] We allowed participants to record as many hours as needed, including more than the theoretical 80 hours representing full-time employment. When participants recorded more than 80 hours in a study period, we contacted them to ensure that those additional hours were valid. In several cases, individual participants recorded more than 80 hours of compliance activity in a two-week period.

- Programs could identify staff who performed tasks relevant to compliance in the five statutory and regulatory areas studied,
- Program office personnel would participate consistently over the course of the study,
- Participants would be able to divide their time into discrete categories (compliance activities), and
- Participants would provide honest input and candid comments explaining compliance mechanisms and perceived burdens.

We believe that these assumptions have been met. We initially signed up eight program offices (the first eight we contacted). Only one of those program offices had systemic participation problems, and by mutual agreement, we suspended its enrollment. The program offices did identify the vast majority of staff whose participation was necessary to properly characterize the programs' compliance activities in the five statutory and regulatory areas studied. Although there was a shakeout period in the first few reporting periods as each program's participant list was refined—and in several cases we added or subtracted a few people at about the midpoint of a program's reporting time frame—our program POCs, division heads, deputy program managers, and program managers generally believed that the right set of program staff was enrolled. Individual participants consistently provided input and responded to prompting through the entire data collection period. After one or two periods to become familiar with our activity categories, individual participants were able to track their compliance time using the activity categories in each area (and "other"). Based on the consistency and detail of most users' input and on the content of the comments they provided, we believe that the data reflect an honest, serious attempt to provide us with the information we requested.

Despite these positive signs, we urge caution in the use of the data. We do not present these data as definitive and precise estimates of the compliance costs at program offices. We feel confident, however, that the data are a good representation of compliance activity, and that general inferences can be drawn from the data with a high degree of confidence.

CHAPTER THREE

Results by Statutory and Regulatory Area

This chapter presents the basic results of our analysis. Most of the data presented in this chapter are at a high level of aggregation; the detailed data can be found in Appendix A. We first present the top-level results and then results by statutory and regulatory area. We end this chapter with a sensitivity analysis to determine the effect of several key assumptions on the results and inferences we draw. As explained in Chapter Two, programs are not identified by names but rather by letters. The brief descriptions of the programs provided in Chapter Two are useful in interpreting these results.

Aggregate Results

The amount of time spent by a program office on compliance activities associated with the five statutory and regulatory areas was less than 5 percent of the total time available to all staff in the program office.[1] This result is considerably smaller than what we expected based on anecdotes from the participating programs, as well as on what seems like a continuous stream of anecdotes from program officials over the last several decades. Program offices obviously comply with statutes and regulations not covered in this study; however, this aggregate result was considerably less than conventional wisdom would imply for the five focus areas.

Figure 3.1 shows the top-level data (in percentage terms) for the seven programs. Each line represents the total reported compliance time in a given period across all five statutory and regulatory areas and all participants in a given program. We have plotted the data against time, as measured by the study reporting periods; there were 33 of these two-week periods to accommodate the different participation start dates. We have also provided a rough indication of calendar dates associated with our study period nomenclature.

---

[1] For the sake of clarity, the calculation proceeded as follows: The reported compliance time in the five statutory and regulatory areas across all participants in a program was summed for each period—this sum is the numerator. The denominator is the total time available to all program staff in a given period; generally, this was calculated as 80 hours per person per period, less holidays, sick days, and vacation. Expressing the level of effort in percentages, rather than hours, normalizes the data for program size and number of participants, making comparisons easier.

Figure 3.1
Compliance Level of Effort as a Percentage of Total Available Hours

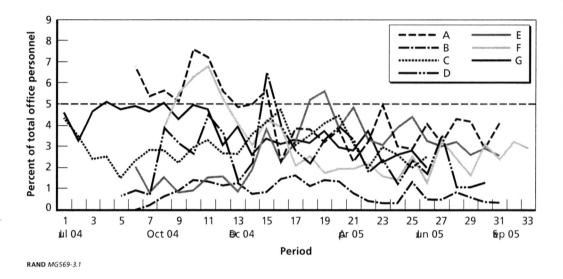

Figure 3.2
Distribution of Time Spent Across Regulatory Areas (1)

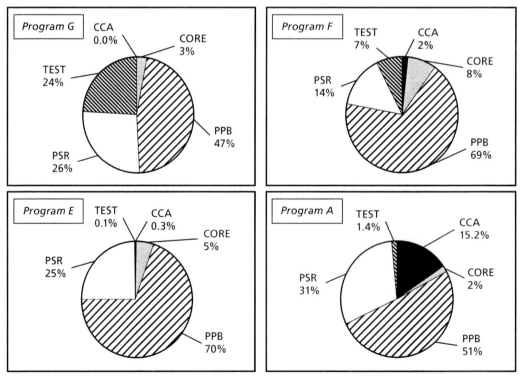

NOTE: Data represent cumulative total over 12-month period.

With the exception of a few peaks, all the lines are substantially under the 5 percent line in each study period. The figure shows the high variability among programs and for a given program across periods. The shape of each program's line and the variability among the programs can be explained with an understanding of the program's characteristics, where it is in its life cycle, and the specific issues being addressed by program staff. Through our numerous feedback briefings to the program offices, periodic conversations with individual participants, and a review of official documentation and publicly available information, we can explain most of the peaks and valleys. We use that information in subsequent sections of this report in support of more detailed analyses. However, our general observation is that the compliance activity level of effort reported is a unique reflection of the program's circumstances. There are few commonalities among the programs. Given the differences among the participating programs, it is remarkable that the reported compliance hours are roughly equivalent when expressed as percentages.

Figures 3.2 and 3.3 show the cumulative total distribution of reported compliance hours across the five statutory and regulatory areas we studied. The programs are

Figure 3.3
Distribution of Time Spent Across Regulatory Areas (2)

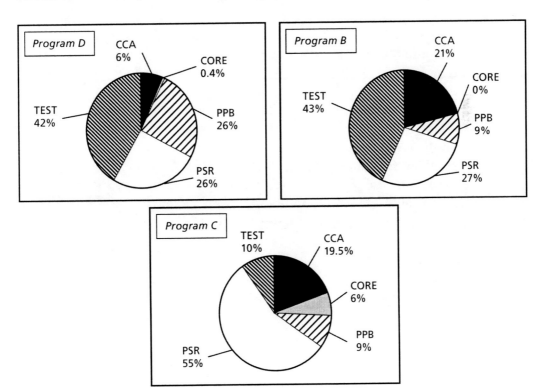

NOTE: Data represent cumulative total over 12month period.
RAND *MG569-3.3*

grouped by the dominant reporting activity; in four programs this was PPB and in three programs it was PSR or Test. Again, each program tends to have a unique distribution based on its specific characteristics and circumstances. Programs A, E, F, and G are dominated by PPB-related activities, while such activities appear less frequent in Programs C, B, and D. Five of the seven programs reported PSR compliance time at around 25 percent of their totals. Programs A, B, and C all have substantial IT components, which is reflected in their reported hours in the CCA area; programs E and G are mature programs in production with few IT-related issues, so they reported few or no CCA compliance activities. Programs B, D, and G were in the middle of substantial test programs, a fact reflected in their test-related compliance hours; Program A's test program was on hold during the course of this study. Although our initial research indicated that Core/50-50 was an area commonly considered burdensome, compliance hours tended to be relatively small across all participating programs. One explanation for this, offered by one program office, was that Core/50-50 compliance requires periodic updating and that cycle was not captured in any of the seven participating programs. This particular program stated that its recently completed Core/50-50 reporting cycle occupied a significant number of program office personnel for a significant time, but it was unable to provide quantitative estimates of that time.

At the aggregate level, few patterns among programs can be observed, reinforcing the conclusion that the reported compliance hours are closely tied to the characteristics of a program, its place in the acquisition life cycle, and the specific issues and challenges facing the program. None of the participating programs faced a milestone decision during the course of the study, although one program did have a DAB-level program review and two other programs were working toward DAB milestones within the next year or so for a major modification representing the future production configuration.

Another important finding was the relative absence of complaints. As described earlier, we asked the study participants to provide two different types of comments as part of their activity reporting. One type of comment was associated with a specific activity performed in that period. The second type of comment was intended to be more general and could address any additional information that the study participant felt we should know. Both types of comments represented opportunities for the study participant to identify activities perceived as overly burdensome—in other words, complain. The participants flagged few compliance activities as overly burdensome. Those activities that were identified as burdensome were most often associated with a new policy or procedure, or some other perturbation in the perceived normal program operating environment. Even then, in most cases, the hours reported against these perceived burdensome activities were minimal. There were many cases in which the participant provided long paragraphs of explanation about how burdensome an activity was but recorded only an hour or two against that activity.

These results are somewhat surprising. The following sections present the data at a slightly more detailed level, focusing on each statutory and regulatory area. Chapter Four examines the data from a different perspective. Using this more detailed level, reporting patterns can be explained and the lack of the expected result can be better understood and substantiated.

Clinger-Cohen Act and Information Management

CCA sets rules for the management of information systems and technology in federal agencies, including the DoD. We were interested in any or all activities undertaken at the program level to comply with CCA or related DoD policy and implementation guidance associated with managing IT and resources, including the Global Information Grid (GIG) and the Joint Technical Architecture (JTA). This includes activities related to the Information Technology Acquisition Board (ITAB).

Overall, most programs reported a level of effort for complying with CCA well below 1.5 person-equivalents per reporting period, on average, which is a relatively small level of effort for any of the participating programs. As can be seen in Figure 3.4, Programs A and C reported the most consistent effort in this regulatory area; as noted above, both programs contain relatively high IT content and both have developmental activities leading to program reviews in which we would expect CCA compliance issues to be addressed. Programs B and D reported some periodic effort, and Programs E, F, and G reported little effort over the 26 two-week reporting periods.

Figure 3.4
Program Office Effort in the CCA Regulatory Area

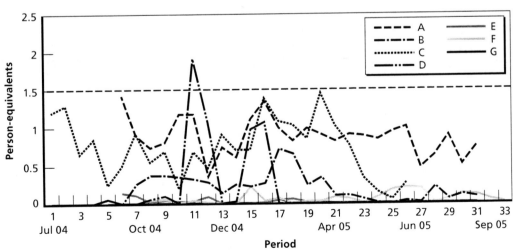

In our data collection protocol, the CCA regulatory area consisted of seven activities that further categorized compliance efforts:

- developing, updating, or revising the CCA compliance briefing;
- developing, updating, or revising the CCA compliance confirmation or certification report;
- developing, updating, or revising the CCA compliance table;
- collecting, analyzing, or presenting information related to GIG or JTA compliance;
- developing, updating, or revising the IA Strategy;
- developing, updating, or revising the system or subsystem registry; and
- completing "other" activities related to CCA, GIG, or JTA compliance.

Table 3.1 shows the average level of effort (in person-equivalents) reported by each program for each CCA activity. Developing, updating, or revising the CCA compliance briefing and the CCA compliance confirmation or certification report required little to no effort by six of the seven programs. The seventh program, Program A, is a young program that has been integrating a lot of IT into its product and that was approaching a major program review during the study, resulting in higher levels of activity than the other programs. Program A reported that program personnel worked consistently in these two activities over the 26 periods. While these activities were continuous over the 26 reporting periods, the level of effort expended within each period was relatively small.

Program C was the only program that expended relatively significant levels of effort related to the CCA compliance table, including GIG or JTA compliance, the

Table 3.1
Annual Level of Effort for CCA Compliance by Program

Program	A	B	C	D	E	F	G
	Average person-equivalent per two-week period[a]						
CCA compliance briefing	0.2	0.0005	0	0	0	0.0008	0.001
CCA compliance table	0.002	0.002	0.02	0	0	0.006	0.001
CCA compliance confirmation/ certification report	0.5	0.002	0.007	0	0.0002	0.003	0
GIG or JTA compliance	0.01	0.002	0.1	0.001	0.003	0.001	0.0002
IA Strategy	0.1	0.1	0.1	0.001	0.001	0.03	0
System or subsystem registry	0	0.0005	0.2	0.002	0	0.0005	0
Other	0.1	0.07	0.3	0.2	0.02	0.002	0.002

[a] This corresponds to the same number of person-equivalents working full time for the entire year. The raw data in hours are provided in Appendix A.

system or subsystem registry, and other IT management–related activities. Program C is a mature program, but it is making significant technological enhancements to its product through a major modification program, which accounts for its CCA activities. The "other" activities relating to CCA, GIG, or JTA compliance consisted mostly of work done on the Information Support Plan (ISP) and the processing of IT waivers.

Programs B, A, and C reported approximately the same level of effort in the IA Strategy activity area, and each program consistently reported data from period to period.

Core Law and 50-50 Rule

The Core Logistics capability requirement and the 50-50 depot maintenance requirement are laid out in Title 10 of the U.S. Code, Sections 2464 and 2466. The 50-50 rule mandates that U.S. government facilities receive half of the funding for depot-level maintenance and repair work for a weapon system. Our research is focused on any activities undertaken at the program level to collect, monitor, or report data or other information regarding the 50-50 depot maintenance rule. Many such activities support the logistics or maintenance sections of the program's ASR or are required to support decisions regarding the support plan for the weapon system.

The Core/50-50 regulatory area required the lowest level of effort by the program offices compared with the rest of the regulatory areas. All but one program office consistently reported well below 1.4 person-equivalents per reporting period over the 26 periods, as can be seen in Figure 3.5. Program B did not report any hours in this area and Program D reported a very small level of effort for the entire 26 periods. As was the case with CCA, the reported data for the Core/50-50 statutory and regulatory area appear to be cyclical for each program, with almost regular peaks and valleys. These cycles are not the same among all programs.

The Core/50-50 regulatory area consisted of five activities:

- developing, updating, or revising the Annual 50-50 Depot Maintenance Report to Congress;
- developing, updating, or revising the Competition Analysis section of the ASR;
- developing, updating, or revising the Core/Source of Repair Analysis section of the ASR;
- developing, updating, or revising the Industrial Capabilities section of the ASR; and
- completing "other" activities related to Core Logistics.

Table 3.2 presents the average level of effort (in person-equivalents) reported by each program for each Core/50-50 activity. Program E reported the highest level of effort in the Core regulatory area.[2] This program was the only program to report any work on the Annual 50-50 Depot Maintenance Report to Congress. Programs E and G reported the most effort working on the Core/Source of Repair Analysis section of the ASR. Even though these two programs had the highest level of effort in these categories, the overall level of effort was relatively low. Both programs support deployed

Figure 3.5
Program Office Effort in the Core Law and 50-50 Rule Regulatory Area

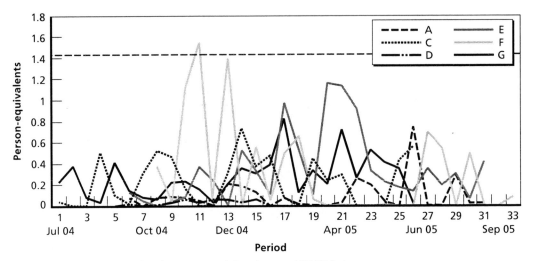

NOTE: Program B reported no hours toward Core Law and 50-50 Rule.
RAND *MG569-3.5*

Table 3.2
Annual Level or Effort for Core/50-50 Compliance by Program

Program	A	B	C	D	E	F	G
	Average person-equivalent per two-week period[a]						
Annual Report to Congress	0.003	0	0	0.0005	0.08	0.01	0.04
Competition Analysis	0.009	0	0.002	0.0005	0	0.009	0.002
Core/Source of Repair Analysis	0.03	0	0.01	0.002	0.1	0.02	0.07
Industrial Capabilities	0.002	0	0.02	0.004	0.001	0.01	0.02
Other	0.06	0	0.2	0.002	0.1	0.3	0.1

[a] This corresponds to the same number of person-equivalents working full time for the entire year. The raw data in hours are provided in Appendix A.

---

[2]   Even so, Program E informed us that it had completed a comprehensive update to the various reports required by the Core Law and 50-50 Rule several months before beginning their participation. Program personnel asserted that reported hours would have been higher had we caught them in their update cycle.

and operational weapon systems with both public and private depot activities that are subject to Core Law and 50-50 Rules.

The level of effort for the Industrial Capabilities section of the ASR and the Competition Analysis section of the ASR was very low.

The "other" activities related to Core Logistics yielded the most effort in the Core regulatory area, with most of the reported hours falling in this section. Program F reported mostly on managing a performance-based logistics support contract and life-cycle management. Program C mainly worked on program planning and information development. Program E worked on program planning with the software maintenance strategy and the 50/50 depot maintenance tasker. Finally, Program G completed various miscellaneous tasks, including training on the 50/50 report, an audit, and compliance-related activity. Interestingly, Program G was informed during the course of the study that it would be subject to the Core Law and 50-50 Rule requirements; the program is looking ahead to a transition from development to production and fielding, making the Core Law and 50-50 Rule activities more relevant as part of program execution.

Program Planning and Budgeting

The PPB area is complex. A single, easily defined statute does not drive the PPB process; rather, it consists of the many different laws, rules, thresholds, policies, and processes that define DoD's financial management environment. The PPB set of activities is intended to capture the time program personnel take to comply with this complex set of statutory and regulatory requirements, as well as to respond to specific requests for program financial or budget information.

PPB accounted for the highest level of effort of all the regulatory areas for four of the seven programs and the second highest level of effort for one of the remaining three programs (see Figure 3.6). The five programs that reported high levels of PPB effort averaged around three person-equivalents per period each over the 26 reporting periods as shown in Figure 3.6. Programs E, G, and D reported a significant number of budget drills of various kinds over the course of the study; all three are large programs in production with relatively large annual budgets. Programs B and C reported much less work in this regulatory area than the other programs over the 26 reporting periods.

The PPB regulatory area consisted of five activities:

- descoping a portion of the program to pay for a funding shortfall elsewhere;
- planning, preparing, or submitting a below-threshold reprogramming action;
- planning, preparing, or submitting an above-threshold reprogramming action;
- conducting what-if exercises to see the effects of changes in funding, schedule, or quantity; and
- completing "other" activities related to programming and budgeting.

Figure 3.6
Program Office Effort in the PPB Regulatory Area

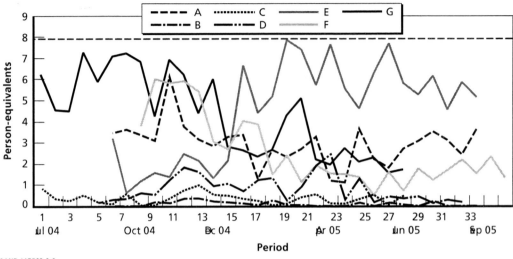

In terms of level of effort, descoping a portion of the program to pay for a funding shortfall elsewhere was reported by five of the seven on a continual basis. Within the descoping subcategory, additional coding of the participants' comments reflects that the most common activity was conducting "funding drills." Table 3.3 shows the average annual level of effort reported for each PPB activity by program. The reported time spent on these reprogramming activities was considerably less than what conventional wisdom and program anecdotes lead one to believe.

Under the activities "planning, preparing, or submitting a below-threshold reprogramming action and an above-threshold reprogramming action," only two programs presented any significant data, Programs F and G. Program F reported a lot of financial management involving its different product lines under these activities. Program G was in the process of a major modification to its product during the study, so a lot of "color-of-money"[3] activities were reported under above- and below-threshold reprogramming.

What-if exercises required the second highest level of effort of the different activities in the PPB regulatory area and some of the highest person-equivalent levels of any activities among the five statutory and regulatory areas. As illustrated in Figure 3.7, five of the seven programs had a significant level of effort in this activity area. Overall, participants specified that they did a lot of funding drills along with the what-if exercises, with about 21 percent of all of the hours attributed to funding drills, according

---

[3]   "Color of money" is a term of the trade denoting the various categories in which money is appropriated. Money appropriated in one category cannot be used to fund activities in another category without approval. Our Phase 1 report discusses the issue in more detail. See Drezner et al., 2006.

Table 3.3
Annual Level of Effort for PPB Compliance by Program

Program	A	B	C	D	E	F	G
	Average person-equivalent per two-week period[a]						
Descope	0.1	0.004	0.002	0.05	0.1	0.1	0.2
Below threshold	0.01	0	0.004	0.003	0.004	0.1	0.06
Above threshold	0.05	0.02	0.0005	0.004	0.004	0.2	0.1
What if	0.6	0.03	0.08	0.4	0.8	0.8	1.1
Other	2.2	0.04	0.3	0.4	3.6	1.3	2.8

[a] This corresponds to the same number of person-equivalents working full time for the entire year. The raw data in hours are provided in Appendix A.

Figure 3.7
Level of Effort for What-if Exercises

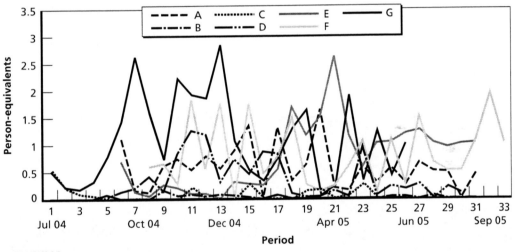

to participant comments. Participant comments also indicated work done in budget preparation and financial management.

The participants reported the greatest effort in the PPB regulatory area as being in "other" activities related to programming and budgeting. This miscellaneous budget category accounted for 68 percent of the total reported hours for budgeting; however, there was a large disparity in reporting among programs in this area. Almost 30 percent of the hours reported in this activity area were categorized as "financial management," 16 percent were either budget execution or preparation, 7 percent were cost analysis, 7 percent were program planning, and 6 percent were hours spent working on issues related to Defense Acquisition Board Interim Program Review (DAB IPR). The rest fell under many other miscellaneous activities. Based on participants' comments, much of the activity in the PPB "other" category was associated with the normal budget cycle or routine financial management.

Program Status Reporting

PSR captures key reporting requirements, both recurring and special or ad hoc reporting, to a variety of sponsors including Office of the Under Secretary of Defense Acquisition, Technology, and Logistics (OUSD/AT&L), Congress, and the [armed?] Military Services, among others.

PSR was the second largest regulatory area in terms of total effort behind PPB. The top-level PSR data are shown in Figure 3.8. All the programs reported time spent in this regulatory area, and most reported that time consistently across the 26 reporting periods. Unlike most of the other programs, Program C reported its greatest effort in PSR, as shown in Figure 3.3.

The PSR regulatory area consisted of seven activities that further categorize compliance efforts:

- collecting data, preparing, or answering questions related to the Acquisition Program Baseline (APB) or ASR;
- collecting data, preparing, or answering questions related to the DAES;
- collecting data, preparing, or answering questions related to the Selected Acquisition Report (SAR);
- collecting data, preparing, or answering questions related to service-specific reports;
- collecting data, preparing, or answering questions related to a Unit Cost Report (UCR);
- reviewing, analyzing, or forwarding a Contractor Cost Data Report (CCDR); and
- completing "other" activities relating to cost, schedule, performance, and status reporting.

Table 3.4 presents the annual average level of effort for each PSR area for each program. Programs A and G reported most of the effort for work related to the APB or ASR. Both programs were revising elements of their acquisition strategy during the study: Program A as it moved toward a major program review and Program G as it made changes to the plan for the major modification. There were few comments associated with this activity.

Four programs reported a notable level of effort on the DAES reporting requirement. The work done on DAES reports was periodic, depending on whether the DAES deadline (a three-month cycle) was approaching.

Figure 3.8
Program Office Effort in the PSR Regulatory Area

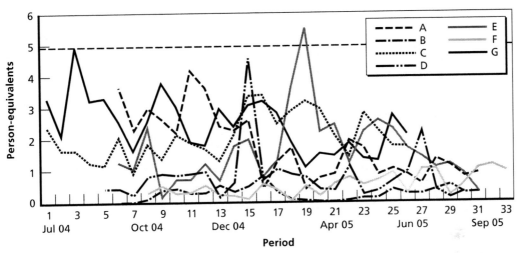

RAND *MG569-3.8*

Table 3.4
Annual Level of Effort for PSR Compliance by Program

Program	A	B	C	D	E	F	G
	Average person-equivalent per two-week period[a]						
APB or ASR	0.09	0.02	0.03	0.007	0.04	0.03	0.5
DAES	0.1	0.02	0.2	0.2	0.2	0.04	0.03
SAR	0.04	0	0.07	0.07	0.1	0.02	0.1
Service-specific reports	0.1	0	0.09	0.2	0.2	0.2	0.4
UCR	0.006	0	0	0.0002	0.0009	0.04	0.03
CCDR	0.2	0	0.2	0.007	0.008	0.03	0.0005
Other	1.2	0.2	1.5	0.4	1.0	0.2	1.4

[a] This corresponds to the same number of person-equivalents working full time for the entire year. The raw data in hours are provided in Appendix A.

Six programs reported effort toward fulfilling the SAR reporting requirement; however, the amount of time reported was small.

Reporting done within the different Services required the second highest level of effort among the PSR compliance activity areas. Some of the more time-consuming tasks reported in participant comments were work on monthly acquisition reports, DASHBOARD, and "smart charts."

Little effort was put into the UCR reporting requirement by any of the programs.

Only Programs A and C reported any significant effort on the CCDR. There were few comments regarding this task.

Other activities relating to cost, schedule, performance, and status reporting accounted for most (62 percent) of the PSR hours reported by the program offices. As can be in seen in Figure 3.9, this activity has a wide range of person-equivalents. Some general activities were noted in the participants' comments, including cost analysis (Programs G, E, and A), DAB IPR (only Program A), information development (Programs C, G, and E), and program reviews (all programs). Various miscellaneous reports were also worked on by the different program offices against which relatively significant hours were recorded: reduction in total ownership cost (RTOC), program office estimate (POE), life-cycle cost estimate (LCCE), earned value management (EVM), contractor performance assessment report (CPAR), and the Cost Analysis Requirements Document (CARD). As in many other activity areas, the program office level of effort and specific activities reported in other activities relating to PSR were a function of the program's characteristics and its current environment.

Testing

The final statutory and regulatory area addressed in this study was testing. By "testing" we mean the level of effort of the program staff in planning, managing, and reporting test efforts rather than the time spent conducting the actual tests or utilizing test results.

Figure 3.9
Level of Effort for PSR "Other"

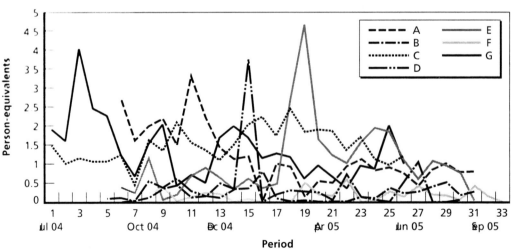

Testing was the third largest category of reported hours among the five statutory and regulatory areas; however, level of effort was significantly lower than for PPB or PSR. Two programs (G and D) reported the bulk of the effort in this area (75 percent), as shown in Figure 3.10. Both are relatively large programs with active test programs.

The testing regulatory area consisted of the largest number of activities. The 11 activities were

- developing, updating, or revising the Annual Report of Director, Operational Test and Evaluation (DOT&E);
- developing, updating, or revising the Beyond Low Rate Initial Production (LRIP) Report;
- developing, updating, or revising the Full Rate Production (FRP) Brief;
- developing, updating, or revising the LRIP/IOT&E Brief;
- obtaining the Live Fire Waiver;
- developing, updating, or revising the Operational Test Plan;
- developing, updating, or revising the Operational Test Readiness Review (OTRR);
- reviewing the Live Fire Test Plan/Strategy;
- reviewing the Requirements Document;
- developing, updating, or revising the TEMP; and
- completing "other" activities related to operational and live fire testing.

Figure 3.10
Program Office Effort in the Testing Regulatory Area

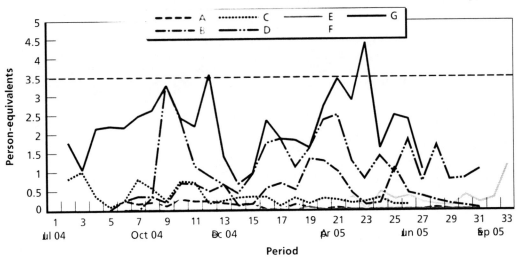

Table 3.5 shows the average annual level of effort expended on each test-related activity by program. The program offices reported little to no work on the following activities: the Annual Report of DOT&E, the Beyond LRIP Report, the FRP Brief, the LRIP/IOT&E Brief, and the Live Fire Waiver. Only five hours total were reported for work on the Beyond LRIP Report for the entire 26 reporting periods, 30 hours were reported for work done on the FRP Brief, and less than one hour was reported for the Live Fire Waiver. These three activity areas required minimal effort on the part of the program offices. Work on the LRIP/IOT&E Brief required a little more effort with 114 reported hours, but more than half the effort was reported by Program A.

The amount of time spent on the Operational Test Plan was more consistent, but the work was mostly done by Programs G, C, and D.

Work on the OTRR was reported mainly by Programs D and G, which accounted for about 90 percent of the total hours reported in this activity. The participants' comments showed that a lot of "test planning" accompanied this regulatory activity.

Most of the hours for the Live Fire Test Plan/Strategy were reported by Program G, with a lot of the activity revolving around test execution and test planning.

Four of the seven programs reported nearly all of the effort recorded in the Requirements Document activity. Much of the Requirements Document work was

Table 3.5
Annual Level of Effort for Test Compliance by Program

Program	A	B	C	D	E	F	G
	Average person-equivalent per two-week period[a]						
Annual Report of DOT&E	0.001	0	0	0.01	0	0.0002	0.01
Beyond LRIP Report	0.002	0	0.0005	0	0	0	0
FRP Brief	0.004	0.003	0	0.003	0	0	0.009
LRIP/IOT&E Brief	0.03	0.01	0	0.00009	0	0.01	0.01
Live Fire Waiver	0	0	0	0	0	0	0
Operational Test Plan	0.01	0.02	0.05	0.04	0	0.004	0.2
OTRR	0	0.03	0.006	0.5	0	0.04	0.1
Live Fire Test Plan/ Strategy	0	0	0	0.03	0.001	0	0.3
Requirements Document	0.02	0.08	0.02	0.09	0	0.08	0.1
TEMP	0.009	0.05	0.2	0.2	0.004	0.1	0.5
Other	0.006	0.2	0.06	0.4	0.0003	0.02	1.0

[a] This corresponds to the same number of person-equivalents working full time for the entire year. The raw data in hours are provided in Appendix A.

done for various product lines within the programs. For example, Program G identified writing an Operational Requirements Document (ORD) for one of its product lines.

Developing, updating, or revising the TEMP required the most effort across the board. All seven programs reported hours in this regulatory activity, although Program G accounted for 40 percent of the total reported hours. Participants commented that test planning, requirements review, and information development were some of the specific activities that went along with working on the TEMP for their various product lines.

The miscellaneous "other" activities related to operational and live fire testing activity areas required the most effort out of all of the activity areas in the testing regulatory area. Hours were reported in this area by all of the programs, but Program G once again reported a majority of the time spent in this area. Some of the activities that were reported in this miscellaneous testing area can be categorized as test execution, test planning, and information development.

Other

Program offices comply with statutes and regulations other than the five areas examined in this study. The Web tool provided an "other statutes and regulations" category in which participants could report activities considered to be burdensome that fell outside of the five focus areas. The reported data are shown in Figure 3.11. Three programs reported a significant level of effort in this miscellaneous category. Program G reported effort toward various training classes and either test or program execution of one element of the program. Program C reported time spent on its foreign military

Figure 3.11
Program Office Effort in the "Other" Regulatory Area

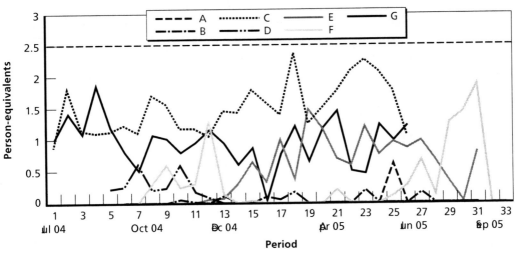

sales program, and about two-thirds of Program E's reported "other statutes" time was associated with the recently promulgated unique identification (UID) policy.

We did not analyze the hours reported in the other statutes and regulations category since these activities fall outside of our designed scope. We did provide the data to the program offices, along with some informal analyses.

Sensitivity Analysis

The data we are reporting here are troublesome in several respects. Despite our best efforts to identify all program office personnel who perform tasks associated with the compliance activities of interest in the study, we could never be sure that we had truly identified and enrolled all relevant program staff.[4] Even with our biweekly email reminders to participants, follow-up phone calls in many cases, subsequent email reminders, and frequent feedback briefings at which we presented the data to date for a program and asked for confirmation, we could never be entirely sure that the data properly reflected a participant's compliance activities. There were quite a few "no work done" responses each period in most of the programs, and it was impossible to validate all of these responses. Thus, we always treated the data as somewhat suspect.

Other indications, however, suggest that most participants took the study seriously and provided honest input (both time spent and comments) for each of the 26 periods. For instance, many participants recorded time in 10- or 15-minute increments. The input patterns of most participants were internally consistent (e.g., they always worked on related activities, or their periodic reporting of certain activities could be verified as legitimate). Most participants provided correct information on sick days and vacations. Perhaps most important, the feedback briefings allowed us to validate the data received to date; in several cases, we updated the data to reflect personnel who might not have been enrolled or who missed a reporting period for one reason or another. Most programs validated the data we showed them; in other words, they looked at the detailed input by user and agreed that the time recorded properly reflected the activities of the preceding periods. At the end of the research, we revisited each program office and briefed them on both their detailed data and the final analysis, including other programs (the same charts are included in this report). Five of the seven program offices agreed that the data properly reflected their actual level of effort, if not their perceptions of that effort. We believe that the two other programs had underreported level of effort. In one case, we appeared to be missing important subsets

---

[4] In one case, one program had reported minimal time spent on CCA-related activities, and validated this at several feedback briefings over a nine-month period. At the last feedback briefing, three months before the program completed its 12-month reporting period, we were introduced to the one person who worked full time on CCA. He was in the program office all along, but was not aware of the study until nine months into reporting. His colleagues apparently were unaware of what he worked on.

of the program office, including test engineers and product managers. In the other case, the discrepancy between reported data and perceived level of effort by the participants was much larger than in other programs.

These kinds of data quality issues are common to survey research. To increase confidence in our conclusions, we performed a series of simple sensitivity tests on the data for each program. These tests and their results are shown in Table 3.6. Most sensitivity analyses change the value of important variables by 10 to 50 percent to determine the effect that measurement errors may have on the results. Because the reported data were so much lower than expected, we used factors of two, three, and four (five, in a few cases) to see what effect their had on the results (compliance time) and our inferences. We doubled the data (multiplying every entry by two) to compensate for missing people and the use of the "no work done this period" responses by participants. In any given period, about half the participants in each program provided this input.[5] Increasing the time spent data by an arbitrary factor of three reasonably covers the possible problem that users were underrecording their compliance time. To address the possible problem that many more program office staff should have been enrolled in the study, we multiplied the reported data by a factor of four, which captured more than 75 percent of program office staff in all but one program.

Our approach intentionally tried to overcompensate for the possible violation of our key assumptions about the number of participants, their ability to record time spent on activities that are categorized somewhat differently than they normally think, and their willingness to sustain reporting over a 12-month period. As Table 3.6 shows, multiplying by factors of two or four will substantially change the reported data. Even

Table 3.6
Sensitivity Analysis of Top-Level Results

Issue	Action	Effect	Result (compliance time as % of total available time; lowest–highest)
"No work done this period" responses not legitimate	Multiply by 2	Doubles the number of users providing data	1.7–8.8
Underrecording; data provided are too low	Multiply by 3	Increases reported data by a factor of three	2.5–13.2
More people should have been enrolled	Multiply by 4	Includes >75% of program office staff[a]	3.4–17.7
Baseline result for comparison	None: data as provided	Not applicable	0.8–4.4

[a] One program is an exception.

---

[5] However, it was not always the same people, leading us to believe that the majority of these responses were legitimate.

under the most liberal (or cautious) assumptions, however, the data still do not show that program office personnel spent an inordinate amount of time on non-value-added or burdensome compliance activities. When using a factor of four, the maximum adjusted compliance time still represents less than 18 percent of the total staff hours available to the program; five of the programs were in the 10 to 14 percent range.

Even compensating for possible data quality problems, the adjusted data cannot be interpreted as indicating that most program office staff spend most of their time complying with statutes and regulations. Chapter Four explores and supports this result from several additional perspectives.

The question of what other tasks program office personnel spend their time on is addressed in Chapter Five.

CHAPTER FOUR

Special Interest Results

Several issues of special interest are addressed in this chapter. These include the proportion of an individual's time taken up by compliance activities, the relative distribution of compliance time between senior and nonsenior program office staff, and the perceived source of the compliance activity. Each of these issues directly addresses an aspect of the overall hypothesis that statutory and regulatory compliance pose an important burden on program management. If that hypothesis is correct, we would expect to see the following:

- a significant proportion of individuals spending most of their time on compliance activities;
- senior program officials (program managers, division heads) spending a significant amount of time on compliance activities, particularly in the PSR and PPB areas; and
- most of the compliance activities perceived as either burdensome or non-value added being generated from sources external to the program, or even external to the service.

The last part of this chapter examines several composite compliance "events" in more detail to try to better understand the link between statutes and regulations, compliance activities, and program consequences.

An Individual's Time

The reported data constitute, on average, less than 5 percent of the collective work time available to program office staff. That metric includes all program office personnel, not just those enrolled in the study. It is therefore instructive to examine the proportion of time spent on compliance activities by those individuals responsible for such activities. An understanding of compliance level of effort at the individual level directly addresses the question of whether many program officials spend the majority of their time on compliance activities, which is the major assertion of conventional wisdom and a fundamental aspect of the hypothesis we are testing.

Figures 4.1 and 4.2 show the proportion of time an individual responsible for compliance activities in the five areas studied spent on such compliance activities for each of the seven participating programs. The charts for each program show the proportion of individual participants in the study who spent differing amounts of time on compliance activities. For example, the upper left-hand chart in Figure 4.1 indicates that 73 percent of the individuals in Program G enrolled in the study spent, on average, less than 20 percent of their available time on compliance activities related to the five statutory and regulatory areas addressed in this study. Only 7 percent of the enrolled participants in Program G spent more than 80 percent of their time on such compliance activities.

The vast majority of participants reported less than 20 percent of their time on the compliance activities we tracked. In practice, this means that most study participants spent a few hours on a few specific activities each period. There was surprisingly little variation among the programs in this regard.

Figure 4.1
Proportion of Time Spent on Compliance Activities by Each Study Participant (1)

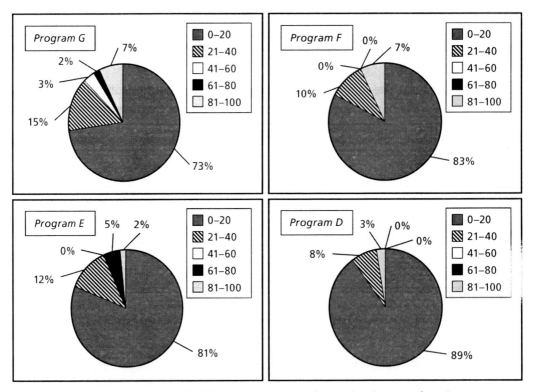

NOTE: Legends show percent of an individual's time spent, calculated as the sum of total hours reported divided by an individual's total available time over 26 periods.
RAND MG569-4.1

A few participants in each program worked full time (or nearly full time) on the compliance activities we tracked. These were mostly lower-level program officials involved in financial management functions (PPB area). But most PSR and test-related compliance activities tended to be periodic, reflecting either standard reporting cycles, ad hoc information requests or planning activities, or the particular life-cycle phase of the program. For instance, the three programs that recorded substantial time spent in test-related compliance activities happened to be engaged in planning, conducting, interpreting, and reporting on test activities.

Senior and Nonsenior Participants

We examined and compared the reported compliance activity patterns of senior and non-senior program officials to see whether there were significant differences in time spent or overall patterns. One element of the initial hypothesis motivating this study was that senior-level program officials spend a disproportionate amount of time on non-value-

Figure 4.2
Proportion of Time Spent on Compliance Activities by Each Study Participant (2)

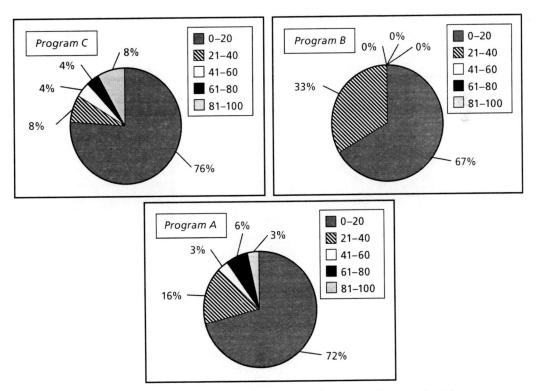

NOTE: Legends show percent of an individual's time spent, calculated as the sum of total hours reported divided by an individual's total available time over 26 periods.
RAND MG569-4.2

added, nonproductive, or burdensome compliance activities, resulting in reduced time available for managing the program. We found little evidence to support this notion.

For purposes of this study, we assumed the senior-level program officials included military officers with ranks at the O-5 and O-6 level and civilians with pay grades at GS-14 (or equivalent) and above.[1] These thresholds capture as senior-level officials the program manager, deputy program manager, product and division heads, deputy division or branch chiefs, and other key personnel with many years of experience. Our analysis suggests that more nonsenior-level personnel are working on regulatory requirements than senior-level personnel and that the amount of hours recorded by these nonsenior personnel is greater on average than the amount recorded by senior-level personnel. This allows senior-level personnel more time to manage the program. This finding again illustrates a definite disconnect between perception of hours worked and actual hours worked. We found that, for the most part, the tasks that might be expected to be performed by non-senior-level personnel (i.e., raw data collection, data input to databases, routine financial management functions) are in fact being done by nonsenior personnel, and that tasks that might be expected to be performed by senior-level personnel (i.e., reviewing final documents) are being done by senior-level personnel.

In the final count of participants, there were 165 nonsenior-level personnel and 87 senior-level personnel. In terms of aggregate hours across all programs, nonsenior-level personnel reported 76 percent of the total hours throughout the study versus only 24 percent for senior-level participants. Within each of the five main regulatory areas, total nonsenior hours (over the 12-month field period) also exceeded senior-level hours, particularly in the PPB and PSR regulatory areas. This can be seen in Figure 4.3.

Table 4.1 shows that the average number of hours worked at the regulatory area level by nonsenior personnel was greater than their senior counterparts. In other words, nonsenior personnel tended to spend relatively more of their available time, on average, performing compliance-related activities in the five statutory and regulatory areas than senior personnel. The greatest disparity between the two levels of the workforce existed in the PPB regulatory area. The average number of hours over the 12 month field period that a nonsenior-level worker reported working on planning and budgeting issues was 247 hours, versus 89 hours per senior-level worker who reported work in this same regulatory area. This result for PPB was driven in part by the relatively larger number of nonsenior personnel who performed financial management activities at or near full time.

Within each regulatory area, the program office personnel separated the different tasks that they did into more specific activities. When analyzing senior versus nonsenior hours reported, for most activities, the nonsenior-level hours are greater than the senior-level hours. There are several exceptions to this statement, mostly in areas where we would expect relatively more senior-level attention, such as reviewing documents that will leave the program office (e.g., TEMP or Requirements Documents) or provid-

---

[1] There were no general officer or Senior Executive Service-level civilians participating in the study at the program level.

ing input to decisions made outside the program office (above-threshold reprogramming actions). The following is a list of activities for which four or more programs reported senior-level hours greater than nonsenior-level hours:

- collecting, analyzing, or presenting information related to GIG or JTA compliance (CCA);
- descoping a portion of the program to pay for a funding shortfall elsewhere (PPB); planning, preparing, or submitting a below-threshold reprogramming action (PPB);

Figure 4.3
Total Senior-Level and Nonsenior-Level Hours by Regulatory Area Across All Seven Programs

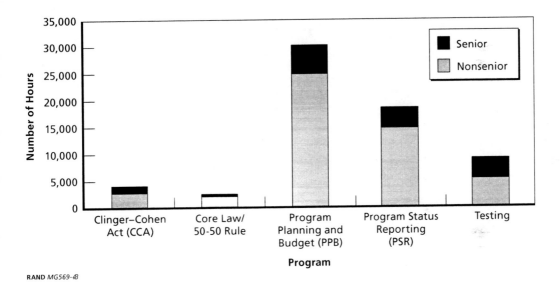

Table 4.1
Average Hours per Nonsenior and Senior-Level Worker by Regulatory Area

	Nonsenior	Senior
CCA	109	63
Core Law/50-50 Rule	64	19
PPB	247	89
PSR	147	56
Testing	152	84

NOTE: The numbers in the table represent the total hours reported in each regulatory area among all seven programs by either nonsenior or senior program personnel over the entire 26 reporting periods, divided by the number of personnel among all programs who reported work in that area. This metric is an aggregate average across the seven programs over the 26 reporting periods.

- planning, preparing, or submitting an above-threshold reprogramming action (PPB); reviewing the Requirements Document; and
- developing, updating, or revising the TEMP.

Senior-level program officials did tend to work on more compliance areas than nonsenior staff. Senior-level officials also tended to spend relatively less time on any one compliance activity.

A different look at the data across programs rather than regulatory areas yields similar results (see Figure 4.4). At the program office level, the level of effort by nonsenior personnel exceeded that of senior-level personnel in all but one program. (Senior-level personnel for Program B had overall effort slightly above their nonsenior coworkers). This can be explained by the fact that Program B had only six total participants, three of whom were senior-level. Additionally, the program office is located in Washington, D.C., where relatively more personnel tend to reach the higher pay grades than in other areas of the country. In terms of average hours per worker reported at the program level, the senior-level workers averaged fewer hours worked than the nonsenior-level workers in all programs but Program B (see Table 4.2). In other words, on average, a nonsenior participant reported 442 hours spent on compliance activities over the entire 12-month study field period in Program A, while a senior-level participant in that program reported 146 hours, on average, over the same period.

Also interesting, at the program-level, is that the number of nonsenior-level participants outnumbered senior-level participants in all but two programs, but that did not necessarily influence the average number of hours reported. Program B, as mentioned

Figure 4.4
Senior-Level versus Nonsenior-Level Cumulative Person-Equivalents by Program

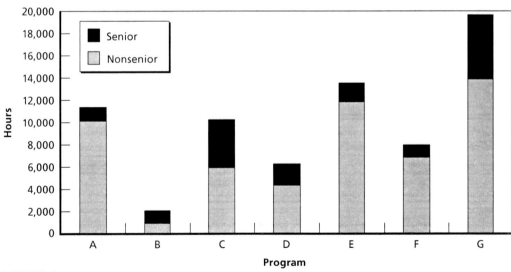

Table 4.2
Average Hours per Nonsenior and Senior-Level Worker by Program

Program	Nonsenior	Senior
A	442	146
B	326	356
C	544	269
D	188	109
E	251	133
F	381	103
G	339	325

NOTE: Data reflect the total hours reported by senior and nonsenior personnel in each program across all five statutory and regulatory areas, divided by the number of senior/ nonsenior personnel reporting. This is the average over the 26 two-week reporting periods.

above, had equal participation between senior- and nonsenior-level personnel. Conversely, Program C had five more senior-level personnel than nonsenior personnel in the study, but reported hours by nonsenior-level personnel were still higher than those by senior-level personnel in Program C.

For Whom Was the Activity Performed?

One aspect of the compliance activity issue concerns the source of the activity, that is, for whom the work was performed. For instance, who requested a particular "what-if" budget exercise? What functional office requested programmatic information? The presumption corresponding to the overarching hypothesis underlying this study is that most of these requests come from outside the program office. Some anecdotes seem to imply that a majority of requests come from OSD functional offices or Congress.

For each compliance activity against which participants reported hours, we asked them to indicate for whom they were performing the work. This was a "check all that apply" style question, meaning that each participant indicated one or more sources for whom they perceived they were doing the work. The results are shown in Table 4.3, which indicates the office that was considered to be the source of the compliance activity. The numbers in each cell are the number of times participants indicated a specific office over the course of the study for each program. Although participants often left this question blank, we were able to fill in some of the gaps based on the nature of the activity indicated and the information in the comments boxes associated with each record.

As with other variables examined in the study, the differences among the programs are explained by program-specific factors such as life-cycle stage, reporting cycles, and special issues or challenges the program was addressing. For instance—

- Programs A, B, and D had specific issues associated with their TEMPs or Operational Test Plans, and thus had relatively more interaction with DOT&E.
- Programs B and F fell outside the OUSD/AT&L oversight process, and Program D was a mature program nearing the end of its production run with no issues requiring OSD attention, hence the relatively few hits against OUSD/AT&L.
- Programs A and E reported relatively higher interaction with their operational user (warfighter) communities.

Perhaps the broadest observation from Table 4.3 is that the majority of compliance activities are initiated by Service-level organizations, including Service Secretariats, audit agencies, functional organizations in the oversight chain, and the PEO and program office itself. The table also shows a relatively permanent Government Accounting Office (GAO) presence at six of the seven programs. The "other" line at the bottom of the table primarily represents activities requested by Congress; this line also includes time spent responding to questions in the RAND study itself.

Discrete Events and Processes

Over the course of their 12-month participation, each program had one or more (usually more) sets of activities related to a particular event, statute or regulation, or reporting activity. We identified some of these activities during the analysis, but some were identified by program officials as something we should track. Although these activities are included in the data already presented, they are worth calling out separately because they provide a different perspective on program compliance activities. We called these sets of activities "nuggets" for lack of a better term. The activities involved generally cut across statutory areas, although the reasons for the activity always had a common focus. Most nuggets had sustained activity over multiple periods; a few larger ones had activity throughout the program's reporting time frame. The nuggets tended to focus specific elements of the program office staff, both senior and nonsenior, on these sets of activities for the duration of the activities. The nuggets tended to be unique to each program. Through participants' comments and discussions with program officials, we were able to identify all individuals who were part of a specific nugget and all compliance activities involved. Based on the comments, we were able to identify and code a more specific set of activities associated with these nuggets. We expected to be able to correlate these nuggets with specific consequences to the program involved.

Table 4.3
For Whom Was the Compliance Activity Performed?

Agency	Program							TOTAL
	A	B	C	D	E	F	G	
OSD	220	63	43	96	128	32	118	700
OUSD/AT&L	58	8	43	4	67	1	33	214
DoD CIO/NII	3	9	13	0	2	0	0	27
DOT&E	17	45	7	13	1	4	8	95
Other DoD	1	2	0	0	4	1	0	8
Service	346	6	121	249	229	127	414	1,492
Service Acquisition/ functional office	74	14	52	48	142	9	44	383
Service CIO/C3I	4	1	4	0	4	11	0	24
PEO/PM	224	196	335	293	202	137	323	1,710
Warfighter community	55	4	23	25	57	2	28	194
Service Test Agency	36	64	27	6	0	5	24	162
GAO	14	0	26	104	31	8	14	197
Unknown	27	1	4	1	18	8	4	63
Other	100	72	62	158	72	38	137	639

NOTE: The OSD and Service labels capture offices within those organizations not otherwise listed in the table, including headquarters or executive offices. The numbers in each cell represent the number of times a user in any of the seven participating programs indicated performance of a compliance activity for that office. NII = National Information Infrastructure; C3I = Command, Control, Communications, and Intelligence; CIO = chief information officer; PM = program manager; GAO = Government Accounting Office.

Among the seven participating programs, only two substantial sets of "nugget" activities involved large numbers of program office personnel over an extended period. These exceptions are detailed separately below. Table 4.4 shows selected examples of the more common nuggets—that is, short-term activities involving relatively few program office personnel. These sets of activities were perceived as burdensome or non-value added by the program office personnel reporting them to us. These were also the nuggets with the highest hours reported against them, other than the two outliers.

The following pages discuss each of the issues listed in Table 4.4.

Program E felt that it spent time on a great deal of program review activities and asked us to track those activities. These reviews, which were mostly external to the program office, included reviews at the PEO, commodity command, service functional staff (acquisition and financial management), and operational user levels. There was

Table 4.4
Selected Activities Associated with Selected Events and Processes

Activity set code	Program	Number of personnel	Number of senior personnel	Number of periods	Total hours reported	Majority of hours
Program reviews	E	26	12	18	873	3 nonsenior: 40%
UID	E	6	4	16	687	1 nonsenior: 74%
Unfunded requirements	G	11	6	17	339	3 nonsenior: 78%
IT approval process	C	7	3	18	253	1 nonsenior: 56%
Congressional reduction of funds	D	7	4	16	181	1 nonsenior & 1 senior: 56%
ISP	C	10	7	18	135	1 nonsenior & 1 senior: 48%
DASHBOARD	D	4	3	14	68	1 nonsenior & 1 senior: 96%

one OSD-level review as well. As shown in Table 4.4, 26 program staff members were involved (roughly 10 percent of the program office total staff), 12 of whom were senior-level officials. The reviews and associated preparation activities occurred in 18 periods; such activity was almost continuous throughout the year. However, a total of only 873 hours were recorded against these activities, and 40 percent of those hours were accounted for by three nonsenior individuals. With the exception of those three, few program office staff recorded more than a few hours per period against program reviews. Despite all the activity, participants recorded no comments indicating that this set of activities was unduly burdensome or a waste of program office time.

Program E was one of several programs chosen to pilot test the implementation of the UID policy issued by OSD during our study, and the program asked us to track that activity as well.[2] The UID policy mandates that every component in a weapon system have a UID code (e.g., a bar code or radio frequency tag) to enable more efficient and effective maintenance and support. Program E is a large, mature program approaching the end of its planned production run, which meant that component, subsystem, or system production lines would need to be modified to tag each component. With thousands of components, program officials felt that this was a major task with significant associated costs. The time recorded was mostly associated with researching

---

[2]   Program G was also a pilot program but did not ask us to track UID activity. Program officials did express the same concerns that Program E expressed. Two other programs recorded a few hours researching the new UID policy and were beginning to assess its impact.

the policy and developing an implementation plan for the program. Six officials (four senior level) in Program E reported 687 hours over 16 periods associated with UID compliance activities; 74 percent of this time was accounted for by a single nonsenior individual (a support contractor). The UID compliance activity hours were spread roughly evenly across the 16 periods. In other words, the new policy generated a sustained new compliance activity. Since the UID plan was neither approved nor implemented during this study, we have no information on consequences (costs and benefits). Most of the work was expected to be performed by the prime contractor and subcontractors for the program, but the program did not generate a formal cost estimate.

Program G recorded a relatively significant amount of time spent on an annual unfunded requirements list activity. The unfunded requirements list activity in Program G was described as an unconstrained exercise to identify needed system improvements not currently funded, generate cost (and budget) estimates for those improvements, and present them to product and program managers. Few, if any, items on the unfunded requirements list are ever funded, according to comments from study participants. Eleven officials (less than 5 percent of total program staff) reported 339 hours against this activity. Three individuals accounted for most of these hours. Six senior-level officials were involved (branch heads and product managers) who reviewed the compiled lists. One individual explicitly indicated this was a non-valued-added activity from the program office perspective. However, there were no impacts on the program other than the amount of staff time spent. Three other programs reported unfunded requirements list activities, but at very low levels (e.g., a single individual in each program recorded a few hours in a short time frame).

Program C indicated to us that a set of activities related to IT Approval was unduly burdensome and non-value added to the program office. The IT Approval process, part of the CCA set of compliance activities, refers to the process a program must go through to get its IT subsystems approved for use. The IT Approval process is designed to ensure compatibility with existing IT systems. Program C is one of the three participating programs that has a significant IT component in both the system hardware/software and mission operations. Specific compliance activities mentioned in user comments included certification and accreditation of hardware/software, preparing the commodity command's IT Approval form, and obtaining waivers from the IT Approval process for select subsystems (12 different subsystems were mentioned). Most of these activities involved the interaction of the program office and commodity command IT functional staff (chief information officer [CIO] office). There was clearly some degree of frustration at the program level; seven program office personnel were involved, and one nonsenior individual accounted for 74 percent of the total hours reported (253 hours). Study participants did not report any consequences to the program associated with the IT Approval process other than staff time spent and cost associated with using the commodity command's "center of excellence" support organization, which specialized in helping programs through the IT Approval process. Processing time could take between 28 and 45 days, according to program staff.

Program D, a mature program nearing the end of a long production run, was subject to multiple congressional earmarks during its 12-month reporting period. The resulting congressional funding reduction caused seven program office staff (four of them senior) to spend a total of 181 hours over 16 periods preparing information, assessing the impact, and performing "what-if" style funding drills to determine the best way to accommodate the funding change. Participant comments described these activities as burdensome and non-value added to the program office. The precise impact to the program could not be determined, but comments mentioned the potential for a production schedule adjustment. The funding reduction itself was relatively small, given the size of the program annual budget.

Program C indicated that the development and approval of its ISP was burdensome and non-value added. Ten individuals were involved in this set of activities, seven of them senior, over 18 reporting periods. No individual recorded more than nine hours in any one period (and only once); most entries were closer to one hour per period. In total, 135 hours were recorded with reference to the ISP.

DASHBOARD is a Navy initiative that attempts to get every program office, PEO, and commodity command to use a standard software and format for reporting program status. It includes the usual standardized reports (SAR, DAES, monthly status reports) and a standard set of displays. Implementation did not involve generating and inputting new data, but it did involve learning a new software program. For that reason, Program D indicated Dashboard implementation as burdensome to the program. Four program personnel (three of whom were senior level) reported time against Dashboard activities. The vast majority of time was recorded by two individuals (one senior and one nonsenior). Interestingly, the pattern over time shows a spike when the new policy is introduced, with comments suggesting a perceived burden associated with the spike, and then relatively few hours reported in any period and no further comments. This pattern, which also occurred in the UID policy in some participating programs, seems both common and reasonable: A new policy is introduced, causing some degree of stress among affected program officials, but once they incorporate it into their routine, the change becomes much less significant.

DAB-level Interim Program Review Activity

Program A was involved in a broad set of activities related to a planned DAB-level Interim Program Review (IPR). Although not a formal milestone decision, the review was intended to cover many of the same topics as a Milestone B decision, including the scope of the ongoing development program, cost, schedule, system capabilities and configurations, and production quantities, among other things. The program had passed its Milestone B several years earlier. However, changes in requirements and operational concepts (both implemented and proposed) had resulted in considerable program turbulence. A review of the program's DAES reports indicated a program that was struggling to reach a stable system configuration and program acquisition strategy, while external stakeholders pulled the program in different directions. The IPR became a decision to restructure and rebaseline the program. The IPR was scheduled for spring 2005, and it did in fact occur as planned; however, several issues remained unresolved and the program was told to come back six months later to revisit those issues. In the same time frame as the DAB IPR activities, the program was managing low-rate production, establishing the first operational base, training users, planning for and conducting development and operational testing, and supporting assets deployed in support of the GWOT.

Senior program personnel clearly felt that the process of preparing for the DAB IPR was consuming the program office staff. Most major documents required at major milestone decision points needed to be updated, including the independent cost estimate (performed by the OSD Cost Analysis Improvement Group [CAIG] based on the CARD supplied by the program office). One program manager estimated that the majority of program office staff (around 100 out of 130) were spending most of their time on DAB IPR preparation activities, including generating the needed information, planning, developing cost estimates, and briefing Service and OSD functional staff, including WIPT, IIPT, and OIPT meetings. Although program office personnel acknowledged that these activities needed to be accomplished to some extent, they clearly felt that the process was overly burdensome and required considerable duplication of effort and information.

Table 4.5 shows the hours reported against DAB IPR activities from two perspectives. The upper portion of the table shows the total hours reported over 26 periods among the five selected statutory and regulatory areas. The majority of hours were recorded in PPB and PSR activities, which corresponds with the specific kinds of activities required for a DAB IPR (e.g., updating documents, creating cost and budget documents, preparing system descriptions). Little time was reported in CCA and testing, although Program A does have a significant IT component and an ongoing test program. The Core Law and 50-50 Rule activities did not come into play in the DAB IPR preparation activities. In fact, the program had only recently been told that it needed to begin incorporating the Core Law and 50-50 Rule requirements into its long-range support planning.

The lower portion of Table 4.5 provides a different perspective on the activities. Based on discussions with program officials and comments in the database, we were able to code activities using functional categories, as opposed to the statutory or regulatory activity labels. Program A reported significant hours preparing cost estimates and related documents, including the CARD. Interestingly, relatively few hours were reported against acquisition strategy or meeting preparation, two areas that would seem critical in the workup to a DAB-level IPR. Similarly, it is important to ask what

Table 4.5
Preparation Activities for DAB IPR, Program A

Area	Total Hours Reported
CCA	1
PPB	1,308
PSR	1,625
Testing	6
TOTAL	**2,940**
Cost estimating (LCCE and EAC)	1,708
CARD	648
Schedule rebaselining (IMS)	414
Meeting preparation (IIPT, OIPT)	101
Acquisition strategy	23
Other	46
TOTAL	**2,940**

NOTE: EAC = Estimate at Completion; IMS = Integrated Master Schedule.

is missing: For instance, where are the hours for test planning (e.g., updating the TEMP and Operational Test Plan), budgeting, and service-level reviews?

Figure 4.5 shows the total person-equivalents charged against DAB IPR–related activities over time. Overall, the data reflect inputs from 12 individuals (four senior) over the 26 periods; three nonsenior personnel account for 73 percent of the reported hours. The reported data diverge significantly from our expectations, given the statement from senior managers that most of the program office staff were spending most of their time on activities associated with the DAB IPR.

Given the missing functional topics we identified, we believe that the reported hours understate the actual level of effort the program office put toward the DAB IPR activities. For instance, the dip in reported hours around period 16 occurs not because the program was ready for its IPR, but rather because the program was focusing entirely on preparation activities to the exclusion of all else, including participation in this study. Using the rationale from the sensitivity analysis discussed above to correct for possible errors, we increase the level of effort by a factor of four: Instead of spending 2 to 3 person-equivalents per period, the program may have spent 8 to 12. That is still far from the 70 to 80 person-equivalents we expected based on comments and anecdotes from senior program managers. Clearly, a significant gap exists between the perception of workload devoted to certain activities within the program and the actual level of effort.

Figure 4.5
DAB IPR Activity, Program A

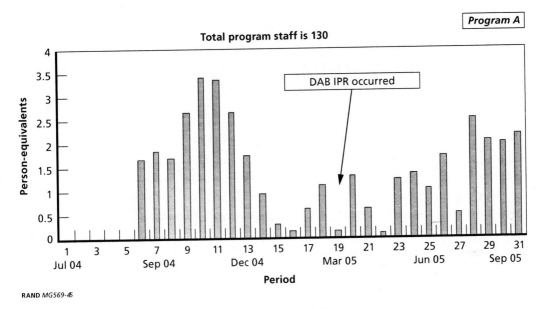

We expected that the DAB IPR activity would have significant consequences for the program, but we found no evidence of such consequences and no reason to believe that any adverse consequences will occur in the future as a result of the DAB IPR activities. In fact, we could argue the opposite: Before the DAB IPR, the program was clearly unexecutable according to information and assessments in the DAES. The DAB IPR activities provided a focus and motivation—a forcing function—for the program to rethink its plan and realign requirements, resources, and time frame. More than a year after the study field period for this program, the program was still not fully rebase-lined, but it was moving in that direction. The rebaselined program will include changes in cost and schedule, but those changes are due to specific program circumstances and not to the DAB IPR per se. In other words, activities associated with the DAB IPR did not directly affect program outcomes and were in fact value added, even though they were perceived as burdensome by the program officials responsible for reestablishing an executable program.

Restructuring a Major Modification Program

Program G is a mature but complex program that includes both current production and development of several sets (packages of subsystems) of upgrades to be included in future configurations. These different elements of the program are called product lines, each led by an O-5 military officer. One of those subprograms can easily be characterized as a major modification program: It includes both hardware and software development, affecting multiple subsystems and resulting in increased weapon system capabilities. Program G is a large program office with 250 personnel and conducts activities in every activity area we tracked. The program manages the full range of funding types—Research, Development, Test, and Evaluation (RDT&E), procurement, Operations and Maintenance (O&M), and military construction.

Of special interest is a set of compliance-related activities that began about the same time our study began. Program G had planned to execute its major modification program using a mix of procurement and O&M funds, reflecting the fact that the subsystems involved had been developed and tested. System upgrades would be accomplished at depots as the fielded systems rotated through their depot maintenance cycle. This plan had been approved and was fully funded. Before the upgrade program was executed, however, a sister program was canceled and substantial funding and personnel were transferred from the canceled program to Program G in support of its major modification program. These funds were RDT&E funds. Along with these transferred funds came the responsibility for completing the development of selected subsystems and related technology and incorporating those subsystems into the package of modifications. Personnel who had been managing these efforts in the canceled program were also transferred to Program G.

RDT&E funds come with different statutory and regulatory requirements than procurement or O&M. These requirements include reporting and accounting systems, but most important, performing both developmental and operational tests on the subsystems being developed using RDT&E funds. This is one form of the classic color-of-money problem that historically has been a source of frustration for program managers. Although one might think that being handed additional funds would be a generally positive event, in this case, the type of funds and associated need for testing caused a complete restructuring of the major modification program. This restructuring of one of Program G's product lines affected every other element of the program.

Table 4.6 shows the hours reported against this particular set of activities. As before, we were able to identify and code data entries as being associated with the restructuring and color-of-money problem based on discussions with program officials and comments in the database. The upper portion of the table shows that most of the reported hours were in the PPB and PSR areas, with a relatively large amount reported in testing activities as well. This corresponds to the kinds of activities we would expect given the situation, as indicated in the lower portion of the table:

- Most of the PPB hours reflected tracking the actual funding transfer and setting up the appropriate accounting procedures for RDT&E funds, "what-if" exercises and other funding drills, reprogramming actions in other affected parts of the program, and other budget-related activities.
- The PSR activities reflected setting up new reporting systems, revising acquisition plans across all program elements, creating the new acquisition plan, and conducting cost analyses.

- The test-related activities included the necessary updates to the TEMP, other test planning, and updates to the Requirements Documents that define the basis for test planning.

The program office personnel who had developed the original modification plan and had responsibility for executing that plan clearly felt that this set of activities was burdensome and non-valued added. One senior official indicated that within one functional branch of the program office, there were "10 people working about full time dealing with this." Conversely, the group of program officials who transferred with the new RDT&E funds believed that the additional testing and reporting requirements were appropriate given the maturity of the technologies involved.

Figure 4.6 shows the distribution of total person-equivalents over time for the restructuring activities. Despite the breadth of compliance activities that the change in color-of-money problems caused, the actual hours recorded are small: On average, less than one person-equivalent reported time against these activities. In a program office with 250 people, that is a fairly small number. The reported data indicate that 18 individuals (nine senior level) reported a total of 1,298 hours over 25 periods. Four program officials (two senior, two nonsenior) accounted for 70 percent of these hours.

Table 4.6
Restructuring a Major Modification, Program G

Area	Total Hours Reported
CCA	0
Core Law/50-50 Rule	40
PPB	540
PSR	518
Testing	200
TOTAL	**1,298**
Cost analysis	274
Color of money	258
Information development	148
Funding drills	132
Program planning	54
Test planning	38
Other (budget, EVM, AoA, ORD)	394
TOTAL	**1,298**

NOTE: AoA = Analysis of Alternatives.

Figure 4.6
Restructuring a Major Modification, Program G

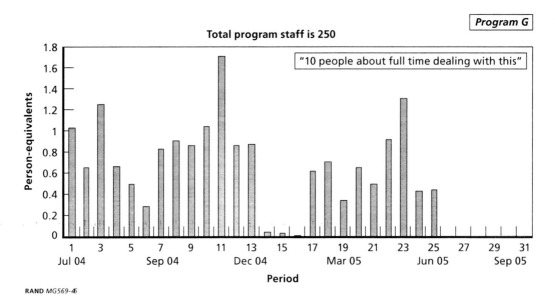

Unlike Program A's DAB IPR discussed above, Program G validated these data as correct, noting that it "sure seemed like more was going on when you're right in the middle of it."

Although the actual staff burden was fairly low from the perspective of the overall program, this change in the color of money used to execute the major modification did have significant effects on the program. The program manager reported that fielding of the upgraded system had slipped by 22 months as a result of the change: nine months for the funding profile change, seven months associated with the color-of-money change, and six months to conduct the newly required testing. The direct costs of the change were estimated at $131 million, including $46 million to construct the needed test articles, $37 million to conduct the operational test, and $48 million in additional overhead due to the schedule slip. In addition, the program needed to buy many more systems in the current configuration to keep the production base warm until testing was complete and production was approved. This is the only example we were able to document in which a specific statute (governing appropriation accounts) had a specific effect on a program's cost and schedule outcomes.

CHAPTER FIVE

Conclusions

Our analysis leads to the following observations:

- The total reported time spent on compliance activities in the five statutory and regulatory areas we addressed is less than 5 percent of the total staff time available to each program office.
- Most program office staff do not work full time on compliance activities in these five areas. In fact, the vast majority of participants reported considerably less than 20 percent of their time as relating to compliance activities in the five areas studied.
- The relative reported compliance workload between senior- and nonsenior-level program staff varies widely among the programs.
- Most compliance-related activities are performed in reference to a Service request or requirement (e.g., program manager, PEO, and Service functional or acquisition staff), rather than OSD, GAO, or other program stakeholders.
- Comments from study participants emphasize process factors (implementation) rather than the intent of a statute or regulation as the underlying driver of the perceived burden of compliance activities. Many of these activities need to be accomplished regardless of whether they are mandated.
- Comments contained few serious statements of perceived burden or non-value-added activities within these five statutory or regulatory areas during the study field period, and reported hours are not correlated with such comments. That is, the majority of comments reflect the participant's view that the activity was burdensome, even if it took little time to accomplish. The explanation appears to be that deviations from an individual's perceived normal job functions are often viewed as burdensome and non-value added.
- There is little evidence of actual consequences to program execution or outcomes as a result of the compliance activities we tracked. We could establish only one firm link between a statute and its associated regulatory processes (Program G and reprogramming) and program outcomes among the seven programs we observed for the 12-month period.

Figure 5.1 summarizes these results with respect to the hypothesis with which we began the analysis. Although programs are indeed governed by a large, complex, and sometimes confusing array of statutes and regulations, and those statutes and regulations do place constraints on program execution, program office staff do not appear to spend a significant amount of their time complying with those statutes and regulations. The reported data suggest that little actual time is spent on compliance activities relative to perceived time spent, and based on the relatively infrequent negative comments associated with reported compliance activities, little of the actual compliance time spent is perceived as burdensome. Lastly, there are few adverse consequences to program outcomes (i.e., cost, schedule, or performance) due to compliance activities associated with the statutes and regulations we studied.

Nevertheless, there remains a significant mismatch between the perception of burden (and cost) and the reported costs (time and program consequences) that we were able to document. At the least, program officials facing what they perceive as non-value-added or overly burdensome work can become frustrated; that frustration should be considered an intangible cost of the DoD acquisition regulatory environment.

But this research—perhaps the most systematic to date that has addressed the statutory and regulatory burden issue—was unable to document any significant costs of that regulatory environment. Program offices do not appear to spend inordinate amounts of time on non-value-added or burdensome compliance activities, and in fact, the vast majority of individuals who perform these activities—a subset of the total program staff—do not spend the bulk of their time in such activities. There are few differences in regulatory compliance workload between senior- and nonsenior-level officials that cannot be explained by the composition of personnel in the program office or by

Figure 5.1
Debunking the Myth

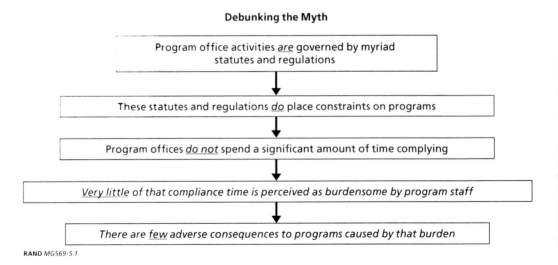

the composition of study participants from that office. Differences among programs can be fully explained by the characteristics and challenges affecting each program.

The perception problem appears to lie more with implementation than with the specific statute or regulation per se. We documented few comments from program officials that suggested that the regulations, or their intent, were invalid.[1] It is the implementation process—that is, the way compliance activities are actually carried out—that appears to be the target of most criticisms and complaints. For instance, program office personnel do not argue that funding should be appropriated in a single account for all purposes, but rather that the process of moving funds among appropriated accounts to respond to unanticipated program challenges is more burdensome than it needs to be. Similarly, no program official participating in this study argued that OSD and Service officials have no legitimate oversight role, but rather that the way in which the information is asked for can be burdensome at the program level.

Comparison with Similar Research

Despite this lack of evidence, the view persists that program offices labor under non-value-added and burdensome statutes and regulations that take time away from critical program management activities and affect program execution and outcomes. During the course of this study, several other independent efforts to document these burdens and consequences were conducted. This section briefly examines the results of these Service-led efforts, which have been widely briefed to senior acquisition officials, who have initiated follow-up efforts to reduce the costs identified by these studies.

One review was conducted by the PEO Carriers office to document the time (staff hours) spent preparing the documentation associated with the CVN-21 Milestone B decision.[2] Time spent by individuals and organizations was tracked from approximately the Milestone I decision (June 2000) through the Milestone B decision (April 2004), a period of 46 months. The data include reported hours by program office personnel, support contractors, the prime contractors and key subcontractors, and Navy supporting organizations throughout the country. Many of the documents tracked were the same as those included in our study, such as the APB, ASR, CCA, Live Fire Test and Evaluation Management Plan, and TEMP. The data also included many documents we did not track, including the ORD, Independent Cost Estimate, Manpower Estimate Report, Naval Training Systems Plan, and Independent Logistics Assessment, among others. Total reported time spent was 245,804 person-hours across all organizations

---

[1] The same is true for PEOs and functional staff we interviewed at the beginning of the study. See Phase 1 report.

[2] The CVN-21 program provided RAND a copy of its summary data file, along with an explanation of methodology.

over the 46-month period. This number is much larger than any program participating in our study; however, the study approaches were quite different. The CVN-21 study included a much longer time period (almost four years verses our one year), many more organizations outside of the program office, and several regulatory areas we did not address. CVN-21 was also working toward a major milestone decision, whereas none of our participating programs were. Thus, the two data sets are not strictly comparable at the top level. Nevertheless, the suggestion here is that the total costs associated with generating Milestone B documents, including organizations external to the program office, is significant in an absolute value sense. Because our study focused narrowly on the program office, we cannot validate this observation based on the data we collected.

A similar study of the Navy's JSOW Milestone C decision preparation was directed by the Assistant Secretary of the Navy for Research, Acquisition, and Development (ASN RDA). This study appears to capture costs at the program office level for required documentation. Required documents were categorized as originating either in the program office or outside of the program office. The study calculated approval process time for some documents (e.g., IA Strategy; Command, Control, Communication, Computers, and Intelligence Support Plan [C4ISP]; System Security Authorization Agreement).[3] The program was required to create or update 38 documents for its Milestone C decision (conducted in December 2004); the study examined 24 of these documents. The study reported that the JSOW program spent a total of 21,918 hours on 24 documents; the study did not report how many program office personnel were involved over what period of time.[4] Only 11 of these 24 documents were considered to be value added by the program office, a consideration we did not address in our study. Because of the known differences in methodology (e.g., preparation activity for a major milestone, different mix of documents, and different regulatory processes tracked), as well as uncertainties regarding other aspects of the JSOW approach (how many people over what time period), direct comparison at the top level is not possible.

At the specific document level, however, some degree of rough comparison is possible between JSOW and RAND since both include and report only program office level of effort.[5] Three of our participating programs (A, B, and C) reported about 250 hours each on their IA Strategy document; JSOW reported 686 hours. Program C

---

[3]   We did not address process time in this analysis, but the document that JSOW personnel took the longest to move through its approval process was the C4ISP at 669 days. In discussion with the program office, however, we found that a single support contractor spent roughly 20 percent of his time shepherding the document and making changes as needed. This anecdote is consistent with the data we collected in our study, in the sense that things are not always what they appear to be.

[4]   See Joint Stand-off Weapon (JSOW) Program, July 2005. The analysis assumed a labor rate of $113/hour and stated most of their conclusions in dollars. For ease of comparison, we use the raw hour reported in the briefing.

[5]   Although the CVN-21 data can be broken down by document, it is not possible to extract only the time spent for program office personnel and their support contractors. Thus, we cannot make direct comparisons.

reported 421 hours registering critical information subsystems; JSOW reported 22 hours. Programs G and C reported 199 and 119 hours, respectively, on their ASR; JSOW reported 100 for its Single Acquisition Management Plan (SAMP), a roughly equivalent document. Program A reported 1,528 hours on its CARD and life-cycle cost estimate combined; JSOW reported 2,000 hours for the same documents. These comparisons demonstrate a rough equivalence between the two studies.

An Air Force effort attempted to identify the most burdensome reviews in the acquisition process by surveying program managers across all Air Force commodity commands. That study did not obtain estimates of the level of effort required for preparation, however. Nevertheless, the study identified WIPTs, IIPTs, "what-if" exercises, and financial budget reviews as processes that require streamlining.[6]

While direct comparison of the RAND study results with these Service-led efforts is not possible due to significant differences in methodology, the limited comparisons we were able to perform suggest that the results are within the error bounds we have established for our own results.

Policy Implications and Recommendations

Because our research did not identify any significant area of non-value-added or burdensome compliance activities driving adverse consequences for program execution and outcomes, we were unable to identify any major statutory or regulatory areas that require immediate attention and reform. Nevertheless, we do have several observations that relate to the policy implications of what we found and recommendations to mitigate some of the perceived burden that was reported.

Our main observation is that there is a significant mismatch between how compliance activities are perceived at the program office level and the amount of time actually spent on those activities. This gap is somewhat troubling and has been identified in prior research.[7] DoD continues to undertake reform and streamlining initiatives, and Congress establishes other acquisition reforms, but the underlying myth of program officials being unduly burdened by statutory and regulatory compliance activities persists. Based on our discussions with program officials, there is no question that they perceive such compliance activities as overly constraining and frustrating. Our data suggest that those compliance activities are not nearly as time-consuming as program officials perceive. Additional research is required to validate our results and, if validated, to determine the cause of this mismatch between perception and actual data on burden (time spent) and program outcomes (cost, schedule, or performance consequences).

---

[6] See Graham, June 21, 2005, and Hassan, no date.

[7] See Smith et al., March 1988.

Additionally, we found that the perceived burden and reported time spent on compliance activities were driven largely by the unique characteristics of each program and the challenges and issues it is currently facing. This argues for a high degree of compliance flexibility, which the governing acquisition policy (i.e., DoD Directive 5000.1 and DoD Instruction 5000.2) has always recognized and encouraged. This flexibility and tailoring should be explicitly incorporated into other specific or functional area policies (e.g., CCA activities, UID policy, reprogramming). Such tailoring needs to be balanced by clear guidance necessary for implementation and sufficient training for program office personnel.

Technical support to program offices would improve the effectiveness of implementation as well as reduce perceived burdens. Such support can be provided by functional offices within the service acquisition staff or commodity command, either using existing organizations or setting up "centers of excellence" to address specific compliance activities. One participating program indicated that such an office within its commodity command greatly helped in complying with CCA, even though it has to pay for that service. That external office can accumulate experience in interpreting and complying with specific statutes and regulations in a way that program office staff cannot (and should not necessarily be expected to).

Not unexpectedly, the introduction of a new policy or procedure causes spikes in program office compliance activity. If that expectation is built into the initial policy implementation process, and if program offices are provided clearer guidance and technical support, the length and severity of the compliance spike can be reduced. The data we collected clearly show spikes in response to new policy or specific changes in existing policy, which then moderate over time and eventually get lost in the background noise of other compliance activities within the program office.

We believe that few efficiencies can be gained at the program office level from acquisition reform or streamlining. In the compliance areas we examined, we did not identify any areas in which policy change or streamlining implementation would save significant dollars in program management funds. Nor did we identify a set of program office personnel who do nothing but comply with non-value-added or burdensome statutes and regulations, and whose jobs would be unnecessary if changes in statutes and regulations and implementing processes were made. The belief that these kinds of savings would result from reform is part of the perception that motivated this research and served as a hypothesis to test. We found little data in direct support of that hypothesis and considerable evidence refuting it.

That does not mean that regulatory compliance is without costs, and some compliance activities may indeed be burdensome and non-value added. It is certainly the case that many program office personnel who have not formally tracked their time spent on such activities perceive that they spend a significant amount of time complying with these non-value-added or burdensome statutes and regulations; however, no evidence supports this perception. It was notable that our study participants began with this view, but ended the study agreeing that perhaps the difference between perception and reality was significant.

The idea of value-added versus non-value-added compliance activities raises an important question: Value to whom? Although some compliance costs may accrue to organizations that perceive such activities as valueless, such as program offices, other organizations may obtain significant value (benefit) from those same activities.

Suggested Areas for Future Research

If program office staff do not spend the bulk of their time complying with burdensome and costly statutes and regulations, then how do they spend their time? This question has several answers. First, program offices respond to other statues and regulations, not all of which were covered in this study. For instance, our data do not include foreign military sales (two programs had separate divisions to handle this), contracting issues (e.g., Federal Acquisition Regulations [FAR] and Defense Federal Acquisition Relations [DFAR]), technical data, or logistics and support (generally a big area for fielded programs). We also did not track training and travel-related activities.[8] There may be other compliance activities may not be listed here as well. Aside from these other potential compliance areas, we believe that the majority of program office staff time is focused where it should be—on managing and executing the program.

This research examined costs at the program office level. These costs are not inclusive of all the costs of statutory and regulatory compliance, however. Costs also accrue at the service and OSD functional staff levels, as well as at service PEO and commodity commands. Additionally, costs will accrue at the contractor level; these latter costs have been widely discussed in the past. To better understand the full costs of regulatory compliance, costs at these other levels should be explored using a similarly empirical approach.

Statutes and regulations also have benefits, which include standardizing content and format, enabling oversight mechanisms, and ensuring that best practices are incorporated into program design, among others. We are aware of few studies that have addressed the benefits side of the equation.[9]

---

[8] Time against all of these areas was occasionally reported and categorized into "Other Statutes and Regulations." Since we cannot be sure what proportion of such activities we actually captured in each program, we did not use these data in the analysis.

[9] Some past studies have at least implied that statutes and regulations have benefits as well as costs; however, we are not aware of any study that systematically examines such benefits.

Program Data by Statutory and Regulatory Area

The following tables provide the raw data used in this analysis. These data have been cleaned and processed according to the methods described in Chapter Two.

Table A.1
User Information and Hours for Program A (By Reporting Period)

	6	7	8	9	10	11	12	13	14	15	16	17	18	19	20	21	22	23	24	25	26	27	28	29	30	31
User Information:																										
Registered Users	26	29	30	30	30	30	30	30	30	30	30	30	30	30	30	28	27	27	27	28	27	27	26	26	26	25
Users Who Provided Data	20	20	20	15	18	15	14	13	14	14	11	13	11	13	8	8	8	12	8	11	13	8	10	9	5	8
Clinger-Cohen Act:																										
Overall	102	71	51	65	85	85	27	51	41	79	108	78	59	79	72	64	72	71	66	69	79	34	50	72	40	60
CCA compliance briefing	0	0	10	2	0	0	0	0	0	48	40	8	9	16	32	16	24	40	8	24	26	0	0	0	0	0
CCA compliance table	0	0	1	2	0	0	0	2	0	0	0	0	0	0	0	0	0	0	0	0	0	0	0	0	0	0
CCA compliance confirmation/ certification report	59	48	24	49	40	56	16	48	24	0	24	40	32	32	24	40	40	16	48	40	40	32	48	56	40	40
GIG or JTA compliance	11	10	1			5	0	0	0	0	0	0	0	0	0	0	0	0	0	0	0	0	0	0	0	0
IA Strategy	2	7	5	4	28	9	9	1	17	29	12	11	18	11	16	8	8	3	10	3	6	0	2	16	0	16
System or subsystem registry	0	0	0	0	0	0	0	0	0	0	0	0	0	0	0	0	0	0	0	0	0	0	0	0	0	0
Other	30	6	11	10	17	16	2	0	0	2	32	19	0	20	0	0	0	12	0	2	8	2	0	0	0	4
Core Law/50-50 Rule:																										
Overall	6	0	6	7	6	4	0	15	13	9	0	6	1	1	0	3	21	16	2	0	60	0	0	25	2	2
Annual Report to Congress	1	0	1	1	2	0	0	0	0	0	0	0	1	0	0	0	0	0	0	0	0	0	0	0	0	0
Competition Analysis	0	0	0	2	2	2	0	5	5	2	0	0	0	1	0	0	0	0	0	0	0	0	0	0	0	0
Core/Source of Repair Analysis	3	0	1	1	2	2	0	6	8	0	0	2	0	0	0	0	0	8	0	0	0	0	0	24	0	0
Industrial Capabilities	0	0	2	2	0	0	0	0	0	0	0	0	0	0	0	0	0	0	0	0	0	0	0	0	0	0
Other	2	0	2	2	0	0	0	4	0	7	0	4	1	0	0	3	21	8	2	0	60	2	0	1	2	2
Program Planning and Budgeting:																										
Overall	249	289	239	245	444	267	245	196	219	239	96	214	164	216	262	89	90	293	174	127	214	220	278	252	192	292
Descope	2	7	4	3	19	49	8	18	24	11	4	0	3	0	0	0	0	17	0	5	0	0	10	0	0	0
Below-threshold reprogramming action	0	0	10	1	5	0	0	8	0	0	0	0	2	0	0	0	0	0	0	0	0	0	0	0	0	0
Above-threshold reprogramming action	0	0	2	1	1	4	23	12	20	26	2	0	2	0	0	0	0	0	0	0	0	0	0	0	0	0
What-if exercise	82	11	8	50	52	37	62	38	59	97	0	105	22	51	133	16	11	48	22	42	20	48	40	38	0	36
Other	165	270	215	190	367	177	152	120	116	105	90	109	135	165	129	73	80	228	152	80	194	172	228	214	192	256

Table A.1—continued

	6	7	8	9	10	11	12	13	14	15	16	17	18	19	20	21	22	23	24	25	26	27	28	29	30	31
Program Status Reporting:																										
Overall	263	177	212	208	157	301	284	167	152	186	34	104	125	33	63	70	157	138	66	78	65	40	111	88	64	71
APB or ASR	4	12	13	14	26	19	23	14	8	22	0	0	8	0	4	0	0	0	0	0	0	0	0	0	0	0
DAES	5	13	25	8	0	7	21	14	38	28	0	0	3	0	4	6	0	0	0	0	6	8	8	0	0	0
SAR	1	4	6	0	0	4	2	3	0	10	8	24	7	5	0	0	0	0	0	0	0	0	1	0	0	0
Service-specific reports	14	3	9	8	21	7	34	10	3	11	3	0	38	3	0	0	0	6	0	4	0	0	3	0	0	0
UCR	0	2	2	2	0	3	0	2	0	0	0	0	0	0	0	0	0	0	0	0	0	0	0	0	0	0
CCDR	40	16	15	0	2	20	30	26	28	29	16	0	0	12	14	24	80	42	0	8	0	0	30	6	0	6
Other	198	128	142	176	108	241	174	98	75	86	7	81	68	13	45	40	77	91	66	66	59	32	69	82	64	65
Testing:																										
Overall	17	14	15	7	20	16	17	11	9	11	0	0	10	0	0	5	0	0	0	0	0	0	3	0	0	0
Annual Report of DOT&E	0	1	1	0	0	0	0	0	0	0	0	0	0	0	0	0	0	0	0	0	0	0	0	0	0	0
Beyond LRIP Report	0	0	0	1	2	0	0	0	0	1	0	0	0	0	0	0	0	0	0	0	0	0	0	0	0	0
FRP Brief	0	0	0	1	0	3	1	3	0	0	0	0	0	0	0	0	0	0	0	0	0	0	0	0	0	0
LRIP/IOT&E Brief	3	4	5	0	4	4	7	4	3	7	0	0	4	0	0	0	0	0	0	0	0	0	3	0	0	0
Obtain Live Fire Waiver	0	0	0	0	0	0	0	0	0	0	0	0	0	0	0	0	0	0	0	0	0	0	0	0	0	0
Operational Test Plan	2	0	2	3	1	1	3	1	2	2	0	0	0	0	0	0	0	0	0	0	0	0	0	0	0	0
OTRR	0	0	0	0	0	0	0	0	0	0	0	0	0	0	0	0	0	0	0	0	0	0	0	0	0	0
Review Live Fire Test Plan/ Strategy	0	0	0	0	0	0	0	0	0	0	0	0	0	0	0	0	0	0	0	0	0	0	0	0	0	0
Review Requirements Document	12	7	5	0	8	5	3	0	2	0	0	0	0	0	0	0	0	0	0	0	0	0	0	0	0	0
TEMP	0	2	2	4	3	3	0	1	2	1	0	0	0	0	0	0	0	0	0	0	0	0	0	0	0	0
Other	0	0	0	0	0	0	3	3	0	0	0	0	6	0	0	0	0	0	0	0	0	0	0	0	0	0
Other Statutes and Regulations:																										
Overall	0	0	0	0	0	0	0	0	0	0	0	0	0	0	0	0	0	0	0	45	0	0	0	0	0	0

NOTE: APB = Acquisition Program Baseline; ASR = Acquisition Strategy Report; CCA = Clinger-Cohen Act; CCDR = Contractor Cost Data Report; DAES = Defense Acquisition Executive Summary; DOT&E = Director, Operational Test and Evaluation; FRP = Full Rate Production; GIG = Global Information Grid; IA = Information Assurance; LRIP/IOT&E = LRIP Initial Operational Test and Evaluation; JTA = Joint Technical Architecture; LRIP = Low Rate Initial Production; OTRR = Operational Test Readiness Review; SAR = Selected Acquisition Report; TEMP = Test and Evaluation Master Pan; UCR = Unit Cost Report.

Table A.2
User Information and Hours for Program B (By Reporting Period)

	6	7	8	9	10	11	12	13	14	15	16	17	18	19	20	21	22	23	24	25	26	27	28	29	30	31
User Information:																										
Registered Users	1	2	2	5	5	5	5	5	5	5	5	5	6	6	6	6	6	6	6	6	6	6	6	6	6	6
Users Who Provided Data	1	2	2	5	5	5	5	5	3	3	4	4	4	4	3	3	4	3	4	3	3	3	5	3	4	3
Clinger-Cohen Act:																										
Overall	4	19	26	29	26	21	22	9	18	15	22	59	46	19	28	7	9	4	1	0	2	1	17	4	9	5
CCA compliance briefing	0	0	0	0	0	0	0	0	1	0	0	0	0	0	0	0	0	0	0	0	0	0	0	0	0	0
CCA compliance table	0	1	0	0	0	0	0	0	1	0	0	0	0	0	0	0	0	0	0	0	0	0	0	0	0	1
CCA compliance confirmation/ certification report	0	0	0	0	0	0	0	0	0	0	0	0	0	0	0	0	0	0	0	0	0	0	0	0	3	1
GIG or JTA compliance	0	0	0	0	0	0	1	0	0	0	0	0	0	0	0	0	0	0	0	0	0	0	0	0	4	0
IA Strategy	4	18	22	14	18	6	5	5	16	10	10	19	28	19	28	7	9	4	1	0	1	1	17	0	2	3
System or subsystem registry	0	0	0	0	0	0	0	0	0	0	0	0	0	0	0	0	0	0	0	0	1	0	0	0	0	0
Other	0	0	4	15	8	15	16	4	0	5	12	40	18	0	0	0	0	0	0	0	0	0	0	4	0	0
Core Law/50-50 Rule:																										
Overall	0	0	0	0	0	0	0	0	0	0	0	0	0	0	0	0	0	0	0	0	0	0	0	0	0	0
Annual Report to Congress	0	0	0	0	0	0	0	0	0	0	0	0	0	0	0	0	0	0	0	0	0	0	0	0	0	0
Competition Analysis	0	0	0	0	0	0	0	0	0	0	0	0	0	0	0	0	0	0	0	0	0	0	0	0	0	0
Core/Source of Repair Analysis	0	0	0	0	0	0	0	0	0	0	0	0	0	0	0	0	0	0	0	0	0	0	0	0	0	0
Industrial Capabilities	0	0	0	0	0	0	0	0	0	0	0	0	0	0	0	0	0	0	0	0	0	0	0	0	0	0
Other	0	0	0	0	0	0	0	0	0	0	0	0	0	0	0	0	0	0	0	0	0	0	0	0	0	0
Program Planning and Budgeting:																										
Overall	0	1	0	17	10	22	29	14	12	10	2	18	4	4	0	0	0	9	0	10	5	0	16	1	0	0
Descope	0	0	0	2	0	0	0	0	0	0	0	2	0	0	0	0	0	0	0	4	0	0	0	0	0	0
Below-threshold reprogramming action	0	0	0	0	0	0	0	0	0	0	0	0	0	0	0	0	0	0	0	0	0	0	0	0	0	0
Above-threshold reprogramming action	0	0	0	0	0	10	16	6	0	4	2	0	0	0	0	0	0	0	0	0	0	0	0	0	0	0
What-if exercise	0	0	0	12	4	5	4	6	4	2	0	4	0	2	0	0	0	0	0	2	3	0	4	0	0	0
Other	0	1	0	3	6	7	9	2	8	4	0	12	4	2	0	0	0	9	0	4	2	0	12	1	0	0

Table A.2—continued

	6	7	8	9	10	11	12	13	14	15	16	17	18	19	20	21	22	23	24	25	26	27	28	29	30	31
Program Status Reporting:																										
Overall	0	3	8	32	32	18	24	41	25	37	67	24	7	6	1	0	5	10	9	29	20	19	33	43	20	23
APB or ASR	0	0	0	3	0	2	10	4	1	8	0	4	0	0	1	0	3	0	0	0	0	0	0	1	0	1
DAES	0	0	0	0	0	8	2	0	0	2	0	12	5	2	0	0	0	0	1	2	0	0	0	0	5	2
SAR	0	0	0	0	0	0	0	0	0	0	0	0	0	0	0	0	0	0	0	0	0	0	0	0	0	0
Service-specific reports	0	0	0	0	0	0	0	0	0	0	0	0	0	0	0	0	0	0	0	0	0	0	0	0	0	0
UCR	0	0	0	0	0	0	0	0	0	0	0	0	0	0	0	0	0	0	0	0	0	0	0	0	0	0
CCDR	0	0	0	0	0	0	0	0	0	0	0	0	0	0	0	0	0	0	0	0	0	0	0	0	0	0
Other	0	3	8	29	32	8	12	37	24	27	67	8	2	4	0	0	2	10	8	27	20	19	33	42	15	20
Testing:																										
Overall	0	0	24	13	53	43	38	47	8	10	52	56	38	108	101	65	24	6	21	80	21	23	17	10	7	3
Annual Report of DOT&E	0	0	0	0	0	0	0	0	0	0	0	0	0	0	0	0	0	0	0	0	0	0	0	0	0	0
Beyond LRIP Report	0	0	0	0	0	0	0	0	0	0	0	0	0	0	0	0	0	0	0	0	0	0	0	0	0	0
FRP Brief	0	0	0	0	0	0	0	0	1	0	0	0	0	0	0	0	0	0	0	0	2	0	4	0	0	0
LRIP/IOT&E Brief	0	0	0	2	2	0	1	0	0	0	5	0	0	2	0	2	0	0	2	0	0	0	0	0	0	0
Obtain Live Fire Waiver	0	0	0	0	0	0	0	0	0	0	0	0	0	0	0	0	0	0	0	0	0	0	0	0	0	0
Operational Test Plan	0	0	0	3	8	2	2	4	1	0	0	2	6	2	0	1	2	2	0	0	0	0	0	0	0	0
OTRR	0	0	0	0	1	3	0	0	0	0	0	2	10	2	0	4	4	2	6	14	0	0	0	0	1	0
Review Live Fire Test Plan/ Strategy	0	0	0	0	0	0	0	0	0	0	0	0	0	0	0	0	0	0	0	0	0	0	0	0	0	0
Review Requirements Document	0	0	8	0	1	0	2	27	0	0	41	40	2	1	6	0	6	2	1	4	5	0	13	1	0	3
TEMP	0	0	0	6	31	8	15	12	4	4	0	4	0	0	0	0	0	0	2	2	4	3	0	3	4	0
Other	0	0	16	4	10	30	18	4	2	6	6	8	20	100	95	58	12	0	10	60	10	20	0	6	2	0
Other Statutes and Regulations:																										
Overall	0	0	0	0	3	1	0	8	0	0	0	0	0	0	0	0	0	15	0	0	0	0	12	0	0	0

NOTE: APB = Acquisition Program Baseline; ASR = Acquisition Strategy Report; CCA = Clinger-Cohen Act; CCDR = Contractor Cost Data Report; DAES = Defense Acquisition Executive Summary; DOT&E = Director, Operational Test and Evaluation; FRP = Full Rate Production; GIG = Global Information Grid; IA = Information Assurance; LRIP/IOT&E = LRIP Initial Operational Test and Evaluation; JTA = Joint Technical Architecture; LRIP = Low Rate Initial Production; OTRR = Operational Test Readiness Review; SAR = Selected Acquisition Report; TEMP = Test and Evaluation Master Pan; UCR = Unit Cost Report.

Table A.3
User Information and Hours for Program C (By Reporting Period)

	1	2	3	4	5	6	7	8	9	10	11	12	13	14	15	16	17	18	19	20	21	22	23	24	25	26
User Information:																										
Registered Users	22	22	22	23	23	23	23	22	22	21	21	22	22	22	22	22	22	21	21	21	21	21	21	21	21	21
Users Who Provided Data	17	18	12	17	14	16	17	13	13	14	16	17	14	17	20	18	16	16	15	15	14	12	13	13	10	12
Clinger-Cohen Act:																										
Overall	86	101	52	68	19	35	72	38	55	14	47	36	62	48	51	112	85	74	67	117	80	60	25	10	4	22
CCA compliance briefing	0	0	0	0	0	0	0	0	0	0	0	0	0	0	0	0	0	0	0	0	0	0	0	0	0	0
CCA compliance table	0	0	2	0	0	0	0	0	0	0	0	1	0	0	0	0	0	0	0	0	35	0	0	0	0	0
CCA compliance confirmation/certification report	0	0	0	15	0	0	0	0	0	0	0	0	0	0	0	0	0	0	0	0	0	0	0	0	0	
GIG or JTA compliance	39	0	0	0	0	0	0	0	0	0	40	0	0	0	0	0	40	11	25	22	0	0	25	0	0	0
IA Strategy	4	45	30	26	0	0	22	0	47	3	0	24	1	2	0	0	0	1	0	0	3	2	0	0	0	22
System or subsystem registry	0	0	0	0	0	0	10	0	0	0	0	0	40	25	43	85	15	57	42	34	22	48	0	0	0	0
Other	43	56	20	27	19	35	40	38	8	11	7	11	21	21	8	27	30	5	0	61	21	10	0	10	4	0
Core Law/50-50 Rule:																										
Overall	3	0	0	41	6	1	25	37	38	11	0	0	22	52	27	39	6	0	37	19	24	0	0	0	30	44
Annual Report to Congress	0	0	0	0	0	0	0	0	0	0	0	0	0	0	0	0	0	0	0	0	0	0	0	0	0	0
Competition Analysis	1	0	0	0	0	0	0	0	0	0	0	0	0	0	0	0	2	0	0	0	0	0	0	0	0	0
Core/Source of Repair Analysis	1	0	0	0	6	1	0	15	0	0	0	0	0	0	0	0	2	0	0	0	1	1	0	0	0	0
Industrial Capabilities	0	0	0	40	0	0	0	0	0	2	0	0	0	0	0	0	1	0	0	0	0	0	0	0	0	0
Other	1	0	0	1	0	0	25	22	38	9	0	0	22	52	27	39	1	0	37	19	23	0	0	0	30	44
Program Planning and Budgeting:																										
Overall	63	22	18	39	11	6	44	1	3	25	50	78	35	35	22	21	4	5	34	45	9	8	25	41	2	39
Descope	4	0	0	0	0	0	0	0	0	0	0	0	0	0	0	0	0	0	0	0	0	0	0	0	0	0
Below-threshold reprogramming action	0	0	0	0	0	0	0	0	0	0	0	0	0	2	0	0	0	0	0	0	6	0	0	0	0	0
Above-threshold reprogramming action	0	0	0	0	0	0	0	0	0	0	0	0	0	0	0	0	0	0	0	0	0	1	0	0	0	0
What-if exercise	39	15	8	3	0	0	1	0	0	0	14	0	0	1	20	1	0	2	10	15	0	3	20	0	0	0
Other	20	7	10	36	11	6	42	1	3	25	36	78	35	32	2	21	4	3	24	30	3	4	5	41	2	39

Table A.3—continued

	1	2	3	4	5	6	7	8	9	10	11	12	13	14	15	16	17	18	19	20	21	22	23	24	25	26
Program Status Reporting:																										
Overall	171	130	134	97	94	142	69	130	107	157	129	136	90	153	241	274	189	210	256	236	165	111	228	175	121	138
APB or ASR	2	2	1	0	0	21	6	0	0	0	0	0	0	0	7	0	0	0	3	1	0	1	14	5	2	0
DAES	46	33	27	9	5	20	30	16	3	11	24	12	21	3	6	0	1	7	32	39	15	1	11	12	11	33
SAR	0	0	0	0	0	0	0	0	0	0	0	3	3	3	18	46	13	2	29	26	0	0	3	0	0	0
Service-specific reports	1	7	4	2	1	6	0	0	1	1	0	0	0	4	54	17	0	1	34	15	0	0	1	28	0	10
UCR	0	0	0	0	0	0	0	0	0	0	0	0	0	0	0	0	0	0	0	0	0	0	0	0	0	0
CCDR	16	9	10	0	1	10	0	0	0	10	2	0	18	18	9	30	40	22	10	0	0	0	60	44	40	0
Other	106	80	93	86	87	86	33	114	107	154	107	108	75	108	148	180	135	179	149	155	151	109	139	86	68	95
Testing:																										
Overall	59	80	32	5	17	17	61	35	18	58	50	14	16	22	25	28	8	22	13	25	20	12	19	25	11	10
Annual Report of DOT&E	0	0	0	0	0	0	0	0	0	0	0	0	0	0	0	0	0	0	0	0	0	0	0	0	0	0
Beyond LRIP Report	0	0	0	0	1	0	0	0	0	0	0	0	0	0	0	0	0	0	0	0	0	0	0	0	0	0
FRP Brief	0	0	0	0	0	0	0	0	0	0	0	0	0	0	0	0	0	0	0	0	0	0	0	0	0	0
LRIP/IOT&E Brief	0	0	0	0	0	0	0	0	0	0	0	0	0	0	0	0	0	0	0	0	0	0	0	0	0	0
Obtain Live Fire Waiver	0	0	0	0	0	0	0	0	0	0	0	0	0	0	0	0	0	0	0	0	0	0	0	0	0	0
Operational Test Plan	0	29	0	0	2	0	1	0	0	2	2	1	1	0	0	2	0	2	2	13	4	2	16	6	6	6
OTRR	0	0	4	0	2	1	0	0	0	2	2	1	0	0	0	0	0	0	0	0	0	0	0	0	0	0
Review Live Fire Test Plan/ Strategy	0	0	0	0	0	0	0	0	0	0	0	0	0	0	0	0	0	0	0	0	0	0	0	0	0	0
Review Requirements Document	4	0	0	1	0	1	0	0	2	2	2	2	2	0	2	2	1	4	4	4	1	0	3	12	0	2
TEMP	55	51	28	4	6	6	28	10	16	46	44	10	15	18	18	10	6	12	7	8	15	4	0	7	5	2
Other	0	0	0	0	6	9	32	25	0	0	0	0	0	2	7	14	0	7	0	0	0	6	0	0	0	0
Other Statutes and Regulations:																										
Overall	62	143	90	88	90	84	84	119	126	84	80	83	101	98	127	126	109	170	100	121	141	169	182	163	123	84

NOTE: APB = Acquisition Program Baseline; ASR = Acquisition Strategy Report; CCA = Clinger-Cohen Act; CCDR = Contractor Cost Data Report; DAES = Defense Acquisition Executive Summary; DOT&E = Director, Operational Test and Evaluation; FRP = Full Rate Production; GIG = Global Information Grid; IA = Information Assurance; LRIP/IOT&E = LRIP Initial Operational Test and Evaluation; JTA = Joint Technical Architecture; LRIP = Low Rate Initial Production; OTRR = Operational Test Readiness Review; SAR = Selected Acquisition Report; TEMP = Test and Evaluation Master Pan; UCR = Unit Cost Report.

Table A.4
User Information and Hours for Program D (By Reporting Period)

	5	6	7	8	9	10	11	12	13	14	15	16	17	18	19	20	21	22	23	24	25	26	27	28	29	30
User Information:																										
Registered Users	12	16	29	34	34	35	35	35	35	35	34	35	35	34	35	35	35	34	34	34	34	33	33	33	33	33
Users Who Provided Data	9	13	12	19	18	20	23	16	16	19	28	21	19	18	19	22	18	13	15	12	15	13	22	9	9	10
Clinger-Cohen Act:																										
Overall	0	0	0	4	8	0	136	86	0	2	70	85	0	0	0	0	0	0	0	0	0	0	0	0	0	0
CCA compliance briefing	0	0	0	0	0	0	0	0	0	0	0	0	0	0	0	0	0	0	0	0	0	0	0	0	0	0
CCA compliance table	0	0	0	0	0	0	0	0	0	0	0	0	0	0	0	0	0	0	0	0	0	0	0	0	0	0
CCA compliance confirmation/certification report	0	0	0	0	0	0	0	0	0	0	0	0	0	0	0	0	0	0	0	0	0	0	0	0	0	0
GIG or JTA compliance	0	0	0	1	0	0	0	0	0	2	0	0	0	0	0	0	0	0	0	0	0	0	0	0	0	0
IA Strategy	0	0	0	0	3	0	0	0	0	0	0	0	0	0	0	0	0	0	0	0	0	0	0	0	0	0
System or subsystem registry	0	0	0	0	5	0	0	0	0	0	0	0	0	0	0	0	0	0	0	0	0	0	0	0	0	0
Other	0	0	0	3	0	0	136	86	0	0	70	85	0	0	0	0	0	0	0	0	0	0	0	0	0	0
Core Law/50-50 Rule:																										
Overall	0	1	0	1	2	4	2	5	4	2	4	0	0	0	0	0	0	0	0	0	0	0	0	0	0	0
Annual Report to Congress	0	0	0	0	0	0	1	0	0	0	0	0	0	0	0	0	0	0	0	0	0	0	0	0	0	0
Competition Analysis	0	0	0	0	2	2	0	3	2	0	0	0	0	0	0	0	0	0	0	0	0	0	0	0	0	0
Core/Source of Repair Analysis	0	1	0	0	0	0	0	2	0	1	1	0	0	0	0	0	0	0	0	0	0	0	0	0	0	0
Industrial Capabilities	0	0	0	1	0	2	1	0	2	1	0	0	0	0	0	0	0	0	0	0	0	0	0	0	0	0
Other	0	0	0	0	0	0	0	0	0	0	3	0	0	0	0	0	0	0	0	0	0	0	0	0	0	0
Program Planning and Budgeting:																										
Overall	13	21	27	41	39	87	129	129	65	74	49	96	105	17	74	152	194	22	102	15	31	28	30	11	23	14
Descope	5	5	5	5	4	2	13	6	17	6	6	2	0	2	0	2	0	0	4	0	6	4	2	0	0	0
Below-threshold reprogramming action	0	1	0	0	0	0	0	0	2	0	0	0	0	0	0	1	0	0	0	0	0	0	2	0	0	0
Above-threshold reprogramming action	0	0	0	0	0	0	4	0	0	0	0	0	2	0	0	0	2	0	0	0	0	0	0	0	0	0
What-if exercise	3	9	15	28	10	60	91	94	22	51	32	69	67	7	72	147	179	20	76	4	16	13	19	0	16	8
Other	5	6	7	8	25	25	21	30	24	17	11	26	37	8	2	2	13	2	22	11	9	11	7	11	7	6

Table A.4—continued

	5	6	7	8	9	10	11	12	13	14	15	16	17	18	19	20	21	22	23	24	25	26	27	28	29	30
Program Status Reporting:																										
Overall	35	32	15	55	69	58	62	75	12	42	324	53	82	64	62	32	29	88	17	27	46	74	151	30	11	25
APB or ASR	0	1	0	0	0	0	0	0	0	0	0	0	15	0	0	0	0	0	0	0	0	0	0	0	0	0
DAES	27	16	3	3	16	11	15	62	0	0	1	8	8	36	15	0	0	8	1	21	28	7	0	2	9	20
SAR	0	0	0	0	0	0	0	0	2	15	20	43	37	6	21	0	0	0	0	0	0	0	0	0	0	0
Service-specific reports	2	7	11	15	21	4	16	0	2	4	35	2	4	0	5	13	25	23	5	2	18	24	80	28	2	2
UCR	1	0	0	0	0	0	0	0	0	0	0	0	0	0	0	0	0	0	0	0	0	0	0	0	0	0
CCDR	0	1	0	0	0	0	12	0	0	0	0	0	0	0	0	0	0	0	0	0	0	0	0	0	0	0
Other	6	7	1	38	32	43	19	13	8	24	268	0	18	21	21	19	4	58	11	4	0	43	71	0	0	3
Testing:																										
Overall	17	26	29	227	186	81	64	53	31	68	126	148	90	113	189	200	100	63	114	78	130	61	116	64	66	87
Annual Report of DOT&E	0	2	0	0	2	0	0	0	12	3	0	0	0	0	0	0	0	0	0	5	0	0	0	0	0	0
Beyond LRIP Report	0	0	0	0	0	0	0	0	0	0	0	0	0	0	0	0	0	0	0	0	0	0	0	0	0	0
FRP Brief	0	0	0	0	0	0	0	0	0	0	0	0	0	0	0	0	0	0	0	0	0	0	0	0	0	0
LRIP/IOT&E Brief	0	0	0	0	0	1	4	4	0	1	0	0	0	0	0	0	0	0	0	0	0	0	0	0	0	0
Obtain Live Fire Waiver	0	0	0	0	0	0	0	0	0	0	0	0	0	0	0	0	0	0	0	0	0	0	0	0	0	16
Operational Test Plan	0	2	5	3	5	0	6	2	3	2	8	5	4	8	2	4	2	0	0	0	0	0	0	0	0	0
OTRR	0	1	20	92	132	0	0	40	0	36	65	83	83	49	0	76	50	4	16	24	54	20	60	62	41	22
Review Live Fire Test Plan/ Strategy	0	0	0	4	13	13	0	0	4	2	2	2	0	10	2	0	2	0	0	0	0	0	0	0	0	0
Review Requirements Document	0	0	0	1	2	5	3	2	4	4	10	9	1	0	34	41	2	0	44	2	4	0	11	0	2	4
TEMP	1	1	0	4	16	17	8	3	4	17	12	11	0	12	6	3	33	33	36	18	29	31	42	2	20	45
Other	16	21	4	124	16	46	46	2	4	3	29	38	2	34	145	76	11	26	18	29	43	10	3	0	3	0
Other Statutes and Regulations:																										
Overall	17	18	49	14	18	42	12	6	0	0	0	8	4	12	0	0	0	0	0	0	0	1	0	0	0	0

NOTE: APB = Acquisition Program Baseline; ASR = Acquisition Strategy Report; CCA = Clinger-Cohen Act; CCDR = Contractor Cost Data Report; DAES = Defense Acquisition Executive Summary; DOT&E = Director, Operational Test and Evaluation; FRP = Full Rate Production; GIG = Global Information Grid; IA = Information Assurance; LRIP/IOT&E = LRIP Initial Operational Test and Evaluation; JTA = Joint Technical Architecture; LRIP = Low Rate Initial Production; OTRR = Operational Test Readiness Review; SAR = Selected Acquisition Report; TEMP = Test and Evaluation Master Pan; UCR = Unit Cost Report.

Table A.5
User Information and Hours for Program E (By Reporting Period)

	6	7	8	9	10	11	12	13	14	15	16	17	18	19	20	21	22	23	24	25	26	27	28	29	30	31
User Information:																										
Registered Users	42	45	45	44	44	44	44	44	45	43	46	48	46	49	45	45	45	45	45	45	44	44	44	43	43	43
Users Who Provided Data	18	16	16	12	16	18	22	10	23	22	23	25	33	36	35	32	26	27	23	25	23	24	24	20	20	20
Clinger-Cohen Act:																										
Overall	10	9	1	3	2	2	7	0	0	0	1	3	3	1	1	0	0	0	0	0	0	0	0	0	0	0
CCA compliance briefing	0	0	0	0	0	0	0	0	0	0	0	0	0	0	0	0	0	0	0	0	0	0	0	0	0	0
CCA compliance table	0	0	0	0	0	0	0	0	0	0	0	0	0	0	0	0	0	0	0	0	0	0	0	0	0	0
CCA compliance confirmation/certification report	0	1	0	0	0	0	0	0	0	0	0	0	0	0	0	0	0	0	0	0	0	0	0	0	0	0
GIG or JTA compliance	0	1	0	0	0	1	0	0	0	0	0	2	2	0	0	0	0	0	0	0	0	0	0	0	0	0
IA Strategy	0	0	0	0	0	0	2	0	0	0	0	0	0	0	0	0	0	0	0	0	0	0	0	0	0	0
System or subsystem registry	0	0	0	0	0	0	0	0	0	0	0	0	0	0	0	0	0	0	0	0	0	0	0	0	0	0
Other	10	7	1	3	2	1	5	0	0	0	1	2	1	1	1	0	0	0	0	0	0	0	0	0	0	0
Core Law/50-50 Rule:																										
Overall	8	4	0	3	7	26	18	0	34	22	8	77	37	8	87	87	70	25	17	12	10	22	15	24	3	32
Annual Report to Congress	8	2	0	0	7	20	10	0	16	6	0	12	19	5	17	0	0	0	0	8	0	12	7	1	1	1
Competition Analysis	0	0	0	0	0	0	0	0	0	0	0	0	0	0	0	0	0	0	0	0	0	0	0	0	0	0
Core/Source of Repair Analysis	0	0	0	3	0	0	0	0	10	0	0	18	12	2	1	16	32	24	17	4	10	10	8	20	1	31
Industrial Capabilities	0	2	0	0	0	0	0	0	0	0	0	0	0	0	0	0	0	1	0	0	0	0	0	0	0	0
Other	0	0	0	0	6	6	8	0	8	16	8	47	6	1	69	71	38	0	0	0	0	0	0	3	1	0
Program Planning and Budgeting:																										
Overall	221	47	82	124	93	173	167	88	139	453	342	408	550	580	427	591	431	357	487	526	443	332	474	356	438	394
Descope	12	1	0	0	0	10	4	0	25	0	17	7	44	9	40	22	8	1	0	0	0	0	0	0	0	0
Below-threshold reprogramming action	0	0	0	0	0	0	0	0	0	0	0	1	0	0	0	0	0	0	0	0	0	4	0	2	0	0
Above-threshold reprogramming action	0	0	0	0	0	0	0	0	0	0	0	0	0	0	0	0	0	0	0	0	3	0	0	0	0	4
What-if exercise	48	10	4	20	14	7	7	0	20	19	20	44	119	91	114	202	90	45	80	72	92	80	80	75	76	80
Other	161	36	78	104	79	156	156	88	94	434	305	356	387	481	273	368	333	312	408	455	349	249	395	280	363	310

Table A.5—continued

	6	7	8	9	10	11	12	13	14	15	16	17	18	19	20	21	22	23	24	25	26	27	28	29	30	31
Program Status Reporting:																										
Overall	87	82	163	14	49	50	96	44	113	133	61	100	255	429	164	189	94	171	202	159	128	89	83	93	65	25
APB or ASR	4	3	0	0	0	0	0	0	0	0	0	0	27	4	1	0	1	0	38	7	0	0	0	0	0	1
DAES	5	5	74	5	0	0	8	2	71	18	0	19	0	0	3	72	0	19	0	8	24	23	0	0	1	4
SAR	4	0	0	3	1	0	8	0	5	54	13	33	15	50	0	0	0	0	0	0	0	0	0	0	0	0
Service-specific reports	43	56	8	2	35	0	10	0	15	18	19	11	26	12	38	25	15	32	12	16	18	26	0	18	6	16
UCR	0	0	0	0	0	0	0	0	0	0	0	0	0	0	0	0	0	0	0	0	0	2	0	0	0	0
CCDR	4	0	0	0	0	0	0	0	0	2	2	0	0	0	0	0	0	0	0	2	2	1	1	0	0	0
Other	28	20	81	5	13	50	70	42	23	42	28	38	188	364	122	93	78	120	152	126	84	38	82	75	58	4
Testing:																										
Overall	0	0	0	0	0	0	0	0	0	0	0	0	0	6	0	0	0	0	0	0	0	0	0	0	2	2
Annual Report of DOT&E	0	0	0	0	0	0	0	0	0	0	0	0	0	0	0	0	0	0	0	0	0	0	0	0	0	0
Beyond LRIP Report	0	0	0	0	0	0	0	0	0	0	0	0	0	0	0	0	0	0	0	0	0	0	0	0	0	0
FRP Brief	0	0	0	0	0	0	0	0	0	0	0	0	0	0	0	0	0	0	0	0	0	0	0	0	0	0
LRIP/IOT&E Brief	0	0	0	0	0	0	0	0	0	0	0	0	0	0	0	0	0	0	0	0	0	0	0	0	0	0
Obtain Live Fire Waiver	0	0	0	0	0	0	0	0	0	0	0	0	0	0	0	0	0	0	0	0	0	0	0	0	0	0
Operational Test Plan	0	0	0	0	0	0	0	0	0	0	0	0	0	0	0	0	0	0	0	0	0	0	0	0	0	0
OTRR	0	0	0	0	0	0	0	0	0	0	0	0	0	0	0	0	0	0	0	0	0	0	0	0	0	0
Review Live Fire Test Plan/Strategy	0	0	0	0	0	0	0	0	0	0	0	0	0	2	0	0	0	0	0	0	0	0	0	0	0	0
Review Requirements Document	0	0	0	0	0	0	0	0	0	0	0	0	0	3	0	0	0	0	0	0	0	0	0	0	0	0
TEMP	0	0	0	0	0	0	0	0	0	0	0	0	0	3	0	0	0	0	0	0	0	0	0	0	2	2
Other	0	0	0	0	0	0	0	0	0	0	0	0	0	1	0	0	0	0	0	0	0	0	0	0	0	0
Other Statutes and Regulations:																										
Overall	0	0	0	0	0	0	4	4	20	44	25	78	27	116	87	54	46	93	59	66	62	62	52	25	1	63

NOTE: APB = Acquisition Program Baseline; ASR = Acquisition Strategy Report; CCA = Clinger-Cohen Act; CCDR = Contractor Cost Data Report; DAES = Defense Acquisition Executive Summary; DOT&E = Director, Operational Test and Evaluation; FRP = Full Rate Production; GIG = Global Information Grid; IA = Information Assurance; LRIP/IOT&E = LRIP Initial Operational Test and Evaluation; JTA = Joint Technical Architecture; LRIP = Low Rate Initial Production; OTRR = Operational Test Readiness Review; SAR = Selected Acquisition Report; TEMP = Test and Evaluation Master Pan; UCR = Unit Cost Report.

Table A.6
User Information and Hours for Program F (By Reporting Period)

	8	9	10	11	12	13	14	15	16	17	18	19	20	21	22	23	24	25	26	27	28	29	30	31	32	33
User Information:																										
Registered Users	14	22	22	23	24	25	26	26	26	26	26	26	26	26	26	26	29	28	28	28	27	27	26	25	26	26
Users Who Provided Data	10	15	12	14	16	11	7	11	10	6	9	6	5	6	4	3	7	7	5	12	7	6	7	7	6	7
Clinger-Cohen Act:																										
Overall	3	4	0	3	1	0	0	16	2	5	0	2	2	6	4	0	7	13	17	14	1	4	10	9	3	1
CCA compliance briefing	2	0	0	0	0	0	0	0	0	0	0	0	0	0	0	0	0	0	0	0	0	0	0	0	0	0
CCA compliance table	2	0	0	0	0	0	0	0	0	0	0	0	0	0	0	0	0	0	0	10	0	0	0	0	0	0
CCA compliance confirmation/certification report	0	0	0	0	0	0	0	4	0	0	0	0	0	0	0	0	0	0	0	0	0	0	0	0	2	0
GIG or JTA compliance	0	0	0	0	0	0	0	1	0	0	0	0	0	2	0	0	0	0	0	0	0	0	0	0	0	0
IA Strategy	0	4	0	3	1	0	0	3	2	0	0	2	2	2	0	0	7	9	13	4	1	3	2	1	1	1
System or subsystem registry	0	0	0	0	0	0	0	0	0	0	0	0	0	0	0	0	0	0	0	0	0	1	0	0	0	0
Other	0	0	0	0	0	0	0	8	0	5	0	0	0	2	4	0	0	4	4	0	0	0	8	8	0	0
Core Law/50-50 Rule:																										
Overall	26	4	78	110	5	90	0	40	4	40	48	5	0	1	0	0	1	0	0	50	44	0	40	0	0	6
Annual Report to Congress	0	0	0	10	0	5	0	0	1	0	8	0	0	0	0	0	0	0	0	0	4	0	0	0	0	0
Competition Analysis	0	4	0	0	1	5	0	0	1	0	0	1	0	0	0	0	0	0	0	5	0	0	0	0	0	0
Core/Source of Repair Analysis	1	0	8	0	1	0	0	0	1	30	0	1	0	0	0	0	0	0	0	0	0	0	0	0	0	2
Industrial Capabilities	1	0	0	0	2	0	0	0	1	10	0	1	0	1	0	0	1	0	5	5	0	0	0	0	0	0
Other	24	0	70	100	1	80	0	40	0	0	40	2	0	0	4	0	0	0	0	40	40	0	40	8	0	4
Program Planning and Budgeting:																										
Overall	270	480	406	421	432	195	178	291	307	114	172	87	150	122	118	111	39	118	54	128	97	130	175	119	167	104
Descope	16	18	16	18	26	10	9	29	0	12	50	20	20	20	8	5	0	0	0	0	0	0	0	5	0	1
Below-threshold reprogramming action	18	19	18	18	17	3	9	11	0	0	0	0	0	20	40	0	0	0	9	10	0	40	40	0	0	0
Above-threshold reprogramming action	22	18	16	17	55	20	29	9	21	0	0	20	0	0	20	20	0	0	2	2	40	0	0	0	0	0
What-if exercise	42	52	19	129	44	113	0	125	37	62	107	20	10	20	50	86	10	78	21	108	53	40	41	87	140	82
Other	172	373	337	239	290	49	131	117	249	40	15	27	120	6?	0	0	29	40	22	8	4	50	94	27	27	21

Table A.6—continued

	8	9	10	11	12	13	14	15	16	17	18	19	20	21	22	23	24	25	26	27	28	29	30	31	32	33
Program Status Reporting:																										
Overall	21	40	19	20	42	15	14	7	46	30	1	40	16	46	62	42	54	66	20	73	80	12	44	82	84	75
APB or ASR	0	4	2	10	8	0	0	0	0	0	0	0	0	0	4	0	20	0	10	0	20	0	0	0	2	0
DAES	0	0	0	0	0	0	0	0	0	0	0	0	0	0	0	40	20	4	0	0	0	0	0	20	3	0
SAR	0	0	1	0	0	0	0	0	1	0	0	0	0	0	0	0	1	0	0	0	0	0	0	10	2	20
Service-specific reports	6	4	14	0	14	0	6	2	45	30	1	0	0	34	10	2	0	22	0	43	45	0	40	0	62	0
UCR	0	0	0	0	0	0	0	0	0	0	0	0	0	0	0	0	30	0	0	0	0	0	0	20	0	40
CCDR	0	0	0	0	0	0	8	0	0	0	0	0	0	0	0	0	0	20	0	0	0	0	0	0	5	15
Other	15	32	2	10	20	15	0	5	0	0	0	40	16	12	48	0	3	20	10	30	15	12	4	32	10	0
Testing:																										
Overall	16	0	22	25	24	16	52	10	16	4	0	32	14	11	26	0	37	19	29	14	10	8	31	15	23	93
Annual Report of DOT&E	0	0	0	0	1	0	0	0	0	0	0	0	0	0	0	0	0	0	0	0	0	0	0	0	0	0
Beyond LRIP Report	0	0	0	0	0	0	0	0	0	0	0	0	0	0	0	0	0	0	0	0	0	0	0	0	0	0
FRP Brief	0	0	0	0	0	0	0	0	0	0	0	0	0	0	0	0	0	0	0	0	0	0	0	0	0	0
LRIP/IOT&E Brief	1	0	0	0	0	0	0	0	0	0	0	0	0	0	0	0	0	0	0	0	0	0	0	1	20	1
Obtain Live Fire Waiver	0	0	0	0	0	0	0	0	0	0	0	0	0	0	0	0	0	0	0	0	0	0	0	0	0	0
Operational Test Plan	1	0	0	0	1	0	0	0	0	0	0	0	0	0	4	0	0	2	0	0	0	0	0	0	0	1
OTRR	0	0	0	0	0	0	0	0	0	0	0	0	0	0	0	0	0	0	0	0	0	0	0	0	0	80
Review Live Fire Test Plan/ Strategy	0	0	0	0	0	0	0	0	0	0	0	0	0	0	0	0	0	0	0	0	0	0	0	0	0	0
Review Requirements Document	2	0	7	11	0	0	16	8	8	0	0	20	10	8	8	0	11	10	3	0	4	3	3	8	2	6
TEMP	12	0	15	14	22	8	16	2	8	4	0	12	4	3	12	0	26	7	26	14	6	5	28	6	1	5
Other	0	0	0	0	0	8	20	0	0	0	0	0	0	0	2	0	0	0	0	0	0	0	0	0	0	0
Other Statutes and Regulations:																										
Overall	20	48	16	22	103	8	0	2	0	0	0	0	0	0	16	0	0	0	8	22	48	10	100	116	148	0

NOTE: APB = Acquisition Program Baseline; ASR = Acquisition Strategy Report; CCA = Clinger-Cohen Act; CCDR = Contractor Cost Data Report; DAES = Defense Acquisition Executive Summary; DOT&E = Director, Operational Test and Evaluation; FRP = Full Rate Production; GIG = Global Information Grid; IA = Information Assurance; LRIP/IOT&E = LRIP Initial Operational Test and Evaluation; JTA = Joint Technical Architecture; LRIP = Low Rate Initial Production; OTRR = Operational Test Readiness Review; SAR = Selected Acquisition Report; TEMP = Test and Evaluation Master Pan; UCR = Unit Cost Report.

Table A.7
User Information and Hours for Program G (By Reporting Period)

	1	2	3	4	5	6	7	8	9	10	11	12	13	14	15	16	17	18	19	20	21	22	23	24	25	26
User Information:																										
Registered Users	47	49	52	53	54	53	53	52	52	50	50	50	50	50	49	47	46	46	46	46	46	45	45	44	44	44
Users Who Provided Data	30	32	31	35	34	26	32	29	28	30	22	22	24	23	20	20	20	29	23	18	18	23	26	21	27	16
Clinger-Cohen Act:																										
Overall	0	0	0	0	4	0	0	0	0	0	0	0	0	0	0	0	5	0	0	0	0	0	0	0	0	0
CCA compliance briefing	0	0	0	0	0	0	0	0	0	0	0	0	0	0	0	0	2	0	0	0	0	0	0	0	0	0
CCA compliance table	0	0	0	0	0	0	0	0	0	0	0	0	0	0	0	0	2	0	0	0	0	0	0	0	0	0
CCA compliance confirmation/certification report	0	0	0	0	0	0	0	0	0	0	0	0	0	0	0	0	0	0	0	0	0	0	0	0	0	0
GIG or JTA compliance	0	0	0	0	0	0	0	0	0	0	0	0	0	0	0	0	1	0	0	0	0	0	0	0	0	0
IA Strategy	0	0	0	0	0	0	0	0	0	0	0	0	0	0	0	0	0	0	0	0	0	0	0	0	0	0
System or subsystem registry	0	0	0	0	0	0	0	0	0	0	0	0	0	0	0	0	0	0	0	0	0	0	0	0	0	0
Other	0	0	0	0	4	0	0	0	0	0	0	0	0	0	0	0	0	0	0	0	0	0	0	0	0	0
Core Law/50-50 Rule:																										
Overall	16	29	6	2	33	10	6	4	18	16	10	2	14	23	21	30	65	8	26	16	58	20	42	32	24	1
Annual Report to Congress	0	0	0	0	2	0	0	0	0	1	0	1	8	19	20	0	22	0	0	0	0	0	0	0	0	0
Competition Analysis	0	0	0	0	0	0	0	0	0	0	0	0	4	0	0	0	0	0	0	0	0	0	0	0	0	0
Core/Source of Repair Analysis	8	6	3	2	3	2	0	2	2	2	2	1	0	2	1	0	1	1	1	16	16	0	42	8	24	0
Industrial Capabilities	2	0	0	0	4	0	0	0	0	2	0	0	2	0	0	0	1	1	0	0	0	20	0	0	0	0
Other	6	23	3	0	24	8	6	2	18	12	8	0	0	2	0	30	42	6	25	0	42	0	0	24	0	1
Program Planning and Budgeting:																										
Overall	423	347	336	559	470	497	577	468	336	483	423	351	406	185	180	184	209	297	399	170	153	216	164	183	110	136
Descope	19	4	6	0	8	0	9	23	12	36	129	78	69	16	10	2	4	6	2	0	0	0	0	0	4	1
Below-threshold reprogramming action	2	0	1	0	0	24	2	30	0	5	2	5	4	0	8	6	0	4	0	11	0	0	2	3	2	0
Above-threshold reprogramming action	0	0	0	0	0	0	12	51	33	43	68	15	8	8	2	4	5	1	1	0	0	0	0	1	0	0
What-if exercise	35	16	13	24	62	101	210	113	58	154	131	149	191	71	37	26	61	89	128	2	18	151	26	98	31	80
Other	367	327	316	535	400	372	344	251	233	246	93	104	134	91	124	146	139	197	269	157	135	65	136	81	71	55

Table A.7—continued

	1	2	3	4	5	6	7	8	9	10	11	12	13	14	15	16	17	18	19	20	21	22	23	24	25	26
Program Status Reporting:																										
Overall	222	164	368	247	264	180	131	174	299	210	128	144	199	156	208	250	223	132	84	118	114	148	108	102	191	170
APB or ASR	22	2	3	7	38	48	41	39	55	98	3	7	11	16	19	112	118	45	22	9	44	62	24	10	17	33
DAES	0	2	0	0	4	3	0	3	8	2	2	29	5	1	0	0	0	0	1	0	0	0	0	0	0	0
SAR	0	0	6	25	5	15	7	6	9	2	37	3	20	4	67	48	2	4	9	0	0	1	0	0	0	0
Service-specific reports	66	37	53	24	32	26	28	21	64	80	35	60	32	0	8	0	3	0	3	30	14	55	8	24	34	56
UCR	4	0	3	3	4	2	2	0	0	0	2	4	16	3	0	0	0	0	0	4	4	1	0	0	0	0
CCDR	0	0	0	0	0	0	0	0	0	0	0	1	0	0	0	0	0	0	0	0	0	0	0	0	0	0
Other	130	123	303	188	181	86	53	105	163	29	49	40	115	132	114	90	100	83	49	75	52	29	76	68	140	81
Testing:																										
Overall	121	82	163	169	176	172	211	222	194	155	242	113	45	63	161	147	146	113	216	270	228	347	130	196	166	85
Annual Report of DOT&E	11	5	0	0	0	0	0	0	0	5	2	0	0	0	0	0	0	0	0	0	0	0	0	0	0	0
Beyond LRIP Report	0	0	0	0	0	0	0	0	0	0	0	0	0	0	0	0	0	0	0	0	0	0	0	0	0	0
FRP Brief	0	0	0	0	0	0	0	0	2	0	0	0	0	0	15	0	0	0	0	0	0	0	0	0	0	0
LRIP/IOT&E Brief	0	0	0	0	0	0	0	2	2	0	0	0	0	0	15	0	0	0	0	0	0	0	0	0	0	0
Obtain Live Fire Waiver	0	0	0	0	0	0	0	0	0	0	0	0	0	0	0	0	0	0	0	0	0	0	0	0	0	0
Operational Test Plan	17	9	6	9	40	48	23	6	48	7	0	20	14	4	32	29	24	5	0	2	16	0	3	10	3	0
OTRR	18	0	0	0	0	16	7	0	7	5	0	45	16	2	20	13	8	0	30	3	0	16	1	0	0	0
Review Live Fire Test Plan/Strategy	22	6	11	8	26	24	91	7	29	16	20	10	2	24	7	6	4	6	0	8	29	6	40	114	114	3
Review Requirements Document	12	24	43	2	10	10	14	12	13	17	4	10	3	2	4	10	0	11	16	16	0	8	3	7	9	2
TEMP	23	5	38	83	20	34	32	10	2	46	16	23	10	5	25	23	50	72	90	65	63	73	51	51	28	10
Other	18	33	65	67	80	40	44	185	91	59	200	5	0	26	43	66	60	20	80	176	120	244	32	14	12	70
Other Statutes and Regulations:																										
Overall	68	108	82	142	96	56	40	73	81	56	64	92	64	40	59	4	62	85	52	93	114	40	38	98	69	97

NOTE: APB = Acquisition Program Baseline; ASR = Acquisition Strategy Report; CCA = Clinger-Cohen Act; CCDR = Contractor Cost Data Report; DAES = Defense Acquisition Executive Summary; DOT&E = Director, Operational Test and Evaluation; FRP = Full Rate Production; GIG = Global Information Grid; IA = Information Assurance; LRIP/IOT&E = LRIP Initial Operational Test and Evaluation; JTA = Joint Technical Architecture; LRIP = Low Rate Initial Production; OTRR = Operational Test Readiness Review; SAR = Selected Acquisition Report; TEMP = Test and Evaluation Master Pan; UCR = Unit Cost Report.

Bibliography

Acker, David D., *Evaluation of the Effectiveness of the Defense Systems Acquisition Review (DSARC)*, Vol. I: *Technical Report with Appendices A and B*, Arlington, Va.: Information Spectrum, Inc., April 4, 1983.

Acquisition Reform Cost Savings and Cost Avoidance: A Compilation of Cost Savings and Cost Avoidance Resulting from Implementing Acquisition Reform Initiatives, AFMC draft report, Wright-Patterson AFB, Dayton, Ohio, December 19, 1996.

ADPA—*See* American Defense Preparedness Association.

American Defense Preparedness Association, *Doing Business with DoD—The Cost Premium*, Washington, D.C., 1992.

Anderson, Michael H., *A Study of the Federal Government's Experiences with Commercial Procurement Practices in Major Defense Acquisitions*, Master's thesis, Cambridge, Mass.: Massachusetts Institute of Technology, June 1997. As of May 3, 2006: http://lean.mit.edu/index.php?option=com_docman&task=doc_view&gid=98.

Carnegie Commission on Science, Technology, and Government, *A Radical Reform of the Defense Acquisition System*, New York, December 1, 1992.

Center for Strategic and International Studies, *Integrating Commercial and Military Technologies for National Security: An Agenda for Change*, Washington D.C., April 1991.

Chairman of the Joint Chiefs of Staff Instruction (CJCSI) 6212.01B, Interoperability and Supportability of National Security Systems, and Information Technology Systems, May 8, 2000.

————, 3170.01, Operation of the Joint Capabilities Integration and Development System, June 24, 2003.

CJCSI—*See* Chairman of the Joint Chiefs of Staff Instruction.

Cook, Cynthia R., and John C. Graser, *Military Airframe Acquisition Costs: The Effects of Lean Manufacturing*, Santa Monica, Calif.: RAND Corporation, MR-1325-AF, 2001. As of May 3, 2006: http://www.rand.org/pubs/monograph_reports/MR1325/.

Coopers & Lybrand, *Acquisition Reform Implementation: An Industry Survey*, report prepared for DoD Service executives, October 1997.

Coopers & Lybrand with TASC, Inc., The DoD Regulatory Cost Premium: A Quantitative Assessment, annotated briefing prepared for Secretary of Defense William Perry, December 1994.

CSIS—*See* Center for Strategic and International Studies.

Defense Policy Panel and Acquisition Policy Panel, House of Representatives Committee on Armed Forces, *Defense Acquisition: Major U.S. Commission Reports (1949–1988),* Washington, D.C.: U.S. Government Printing Office, 1988.

DoDI—*See* U.S. Department of Defense Instruction.

Drezner, Jeffrey A., and Giles K. Smith, *An Analysis of Weapon System Acquisition Schedules,* Santa Monica, Calif.: RAND Corporation, R-3937-ACQ, 1990.

Drezner, Jeffrey A., Raj Raman, Irv Blickstein, John Ablard, Melissa Bradley, Brent Eastwood, Maria Falvo, Dikla Gavrieli, Monica Hertzman, Darryl Lenhardt, and Megan McKernan, *Measuring the Statutory and Regulatory Constraints on DoD Acquisition: Research Design for An Empirical Study,* Santa Monica, Calif.: RAND Corporation, TR-347-OSD, 2006. As of May 3, 2006: http://www.rand.org/pubs/technical_reports/TR347/.

Ferrara, Joe, "DoD's 5000 Documents: Evolution and Change in Defense Acquisition Policy," *Acquisition Review Quarterly,* Fall 1996, pp. 109–130. As of May 3, 2006: http://www.dau.mil/pubs/arq/94arq/ferrar.pdf.

GAO—*See* U.S. General Accounting Office.

Glossary of Defense Acquisition Acronyms and Terms, 11th ed., Fort Belvoir, Va.: Defense Acquisition University Press, September 2003. As of May 3, 2006: http://www.jpeocbd.osd.mil/documents/DefenseAcroynms.pdf. Current version (12th ed., July 2005). As of May 3, 2006: http://www.dau.mil/pubs/glossary/12th_Glossary_2005.pdf.

Graham, Scott, AFMC/XRQ, Streamline Program Oversight, TIG briefing, June 21, 2005.

Hanks, Christopher H., Elliot I. Axelband, Shuna Lindsay, Rehan Malik, and Brett D. Steele, *Reexamining Military Acquisition Reform: Are We There Yet?* Santa Monica, Calif.: RAND Corporation, MG-291-A, 2005. As of May 3, 2006: http://www.rand.org/pubs/monographs/MG291/.

Hassan, Janet, Secretary of the Air Force/Acquisitions SAF/AQ Acquisition Chief Process Office, Acquisition Process Enterprise Value Stream Mapping Assessment (EVSMA), briefing, no date.

Honeywell, *Defense Acquisition Improvement Study,* May 1986.

Institute for Defense Analyses, *Role of OSD in the Acquisition Process,* Alexandria, Va., 1991.

Joint Stand-off Weapon (JSOW) Program, C Milestone III Program Documentation, briefing prepared for Hon. John Young, ASN(RDA), July 2005.

Krikorian, George K., "DoD's Cost Premium Thirty to Fifty Percent, National Defense," *Journal of American Defense Preparedness Association,* September 1992.

Lorell, Mark A., and John C. Graser, *An Overview of Acquisition Reform Cost Savings Estimates,* Santa Monica, Calif.: RAND Corporation, MR-1329-AF, 2001. As of May 3, 2006: http://www.rand.org/pubs/monograph_reports/MR1329/.

Lorell, Mark A., Julia F. Lowell, Michael Kennedy, and Hugh P. Levaux, *Cheaper, Faster, Better? Commercial Approaches to Weapons Acquisition,* Santa Monica, Calif.: RAND Corporation, MR-1147-AF, 2000. As of May 3, 2006: http://www.rand.org/pubs/monograph_reports/MR1147/.

NORCOM, *Activity-Based Cost Analysis of Cost of DoD Requirements and Cost of Capacity: Executive Summary,* May 1994.

Office of the Assistant Secretary of the Air Force, Acquisition, *Acquisition Reform Success Story: Wind Corrected Munitions Dispenser (WCMD),* June 12, 1997.

Office of the Deputy Under Secretary of Defense, Acquisition Reform, *Single Process Initiative, Acquisition Reform Acceleration Day Stand-Down,* 1996a.

————, Acquisition Reform, *Cost as an Independent Variable: Stand-Down Acquisition Reform Acceleration Day,* May 1996b.

————, Acquisition Reform, Defense Acquisition Pilot Programs, Pilot Program Consulting Group on Metrics, *Celebrating Success: Forging the Future,* 1997a.

————, Acquisition Reform, Pilot Program Consulting Group, *PPCG 1997 Compendium of Pilot Program Reports,* 1997b.

Office of the Under Secretary of Defense, Acquisition and Technology, *Report of the Defense Science Board Task Force on Acquisition Reform,* Washington, D.C.: Defense Science Board, 1993.

————, Acquisition and Technology, Acquisition Reform Senior Steering Group, DoD Regulatory Cost Premium Group, *Updated Compendium of Office of Primary Responsibility (OPR) Reports,* June 1996.

————, Acquisition and Technology, Acquisition Reform Benchmarking Group, *1997 Final Report,* June 30, 1997.

————, Acquisition and Technology, *Report of the Defense Science Board Task Force on Acquisition Reform, Phase IV,* Washington, D.C.: Defense Science Board, July 1999. As of May 3, 2006: http://www.acq.osd.mil/dsb/reports/acqreformfour.pdf.

OUSD—*See* Office of the Under Secretary of Defense.

Packard Commission, *Reports of the President's Blue Ribbon Commission on Defense Management, Final Report to the President: A Quest for Excellence,* Washington, D.C., June 1986. As of May 3, 2006: http://www.ndu.edu/library/pbrc/pbrc.html.

Perry, William J., Secretary of Defense, "Acquisition Reform—Mandate for Change," memorandum, February 1994.

————, "Specifications and Standards—A New Way of Doing Business," memorandum, June 29, 1994.

Public Law 104-106, National Defense Authorization Act for Fiscal Year 1996, 104th Congress, February 10, 1996.

Public Law 107-248, Department of Defense Appropriations Act, 2003, 107th Congress, October 23, 2002.

Rich, Michael, Edmund Dews, and C. L. Batten, *Improving the Military Acquisition Process: Lessons from RAND Research,* Santa Monica, Calif.: RAND Corporation, R-3373-AF/RC, 1986. As of May 3, 2006: http://www.rand.org/pubs/reports/R3373/.

Rogers, Edward W., and Robert P. Birmingham, "A Ten-Year Review of the Vision for Transforming the Defense Acquisition System," *Defense Acquisition Review Quarterly,* January–April 2004, pp. 36–61. As of May 3, 2006: http://www.dau.mil/pubs/arq/2004arq/Rogers.pdf.

Rush, Benjamin C., "Cost as an Independent Variable: Concepts and Risks," *Acquisition Review Quarterly,* Spring 1997, pp. 161–172. As of May 3, 2006: http://www.dau.mil/pubs/arq/97arq/rus.pdf.

Schank, John, Kathi Webb, Eugene Bryton, and Jerry Sollinger, Analysis of Service-Reported Acquisition Reform Reductions: An Annotated Briefing, Santa Monica, Calif.: RAND Corporation, unpublished research, September 1996.

Secretary of the Navy Instruction (SECNAVINST) 5000.2B, Implementation of Mandatory Procedures for Major and Non-Major Defense Acquisition Programs and Major and Non-Major Information Technology Acquisition Programs, December 6, 1996.

Smith, Giles K., Jeffrey A. Drezner, William C. Martel, James J. Milanese, W. E. Mooz, and E. C.
River, *A Preliminary Perspective on Regulatory Activities and Effects in Weapons Acquisition,* Santa
Monica, Calif.: RAND Corporation, R-3578-ACQ, 1988.

Sylvester, Richard K., and Joseph A. Ferrara, "Conflict and Ambiguity: Implementing Evolutionary
Acquisition," *Acquisition Review Quarterly,* Winter 2003. As of May 3, 2006:
http://www.dau.mil/pubs/arq/2003arq/Sylvesterwt3.pdf.

United States Code, Title 10, Armed Forces, Chapter 4, Office of the Secretary of Defense, Section
139, Director of Operational Test and Evaluation, January 19, 2004.

———, Title 10, Armed Forces, Chapter 137, Procurement Generally, Section 2302, Definitions,
January 19, 2004.

———, Title 10, Armed Forces, Chapter 139, Research and Development, Section 2366, Major
Systems and Munitions Programs: Survivability, Testing and Lethality Testing Required Before
Full-Scale Production, January 19, 2004.

———, Title 10, Armed Forces, Chapter 141, Miscellaneous Procurement Provisions, Section
2399, Operational Test and Evaluation of Defense Acquisition Programs, January 19, 2004.

———, Title 10, Armed Forces, Chapter 144, Major Defense Acquisition Programs, Section 2440,
Technology and Industrial Base Plans, January 19, 2004.

———, Title 10, Armed Forces, Chapter 146, Contracting for Performance of Civilian Commercial
or Industrial Type Functions, Section 2464, Core Logistics Capabilities, January 19, 2004.

———, Title 10, Armed Forces, Chapter 146, Contracting for Performance of Civilian
Commercial or Industrial Type Functions, Section 2466, Limitations on the Performance of
Depot-Level Maintenance of Materiel, January 19, 2004.

U.S. Congress, House of Representatives Committee on Armed Forces, *Future of the Defense
Industrial Base: Report of the Structure of the U.S. Defense Industrial Base Panel,* 1992.

U.S. Congress, Office of Technology Assessment, *Holding the Edge: Maintaining the Defense
Technology Base,* Vol. 2: *Appendixes,* Washington D.C.: U.S. Government Printing Office,
OTA-ISC-432, April 1989.

———, *Redesigning Defense: Planning the Transition to the Future U.S. Defense Industrial Base,*
Washington, D.C.: U.S. Government Printing Office, OTA-ISC-500, July 1991.

U.S. Department of Defense, *The Defense Transformation for the 21st Century,* Washington, D.C.:
General Council of the Department of Defense, April 10, 2003. As of May 3, 2006:
http://www.oft.osd.mil/library/library_files/document_131_Dod%20Transformation%20Act%20.pdf.

———, *Report of the Defense Science Board Task Force on Management Oversight in Acquisition
Organizations,* Washington, D.C.: Office of the Under Secretary of Defense for Acquisition,
Technology, and Logistics, March 2005. As of May 3, 2006:
http://www.acq.osd.mil/dsb/reports/2005-03-MOAO_Report_Final.pdf.

U.S. Department of Defense Directive (DoDD) 5000.1, The Defense Acquisition System, May 12,
2003.

U.S. Department of Defense, Defense Systems Management College, *Streamlining Defense Acquisition Laws, Executive Summary: Report of the DoD Acquisition Law Advisory Panel,* Fort Belvoir, Va.:
Defense Systems Management College Press, March 1993.

U.S. Department of Defense Instruction (DoDI) 5000.2, Operation of the Defense Acquisition System, May 12, 2003.

U.S. General Accounting Office, *Acquisition Reform: Efforts to Reduce the Cost to Manage and Over-See DoD Contracts,* report to congressional committees, Washington, D.C., GAO/NSIAD-96-106, April 1996. As of May 3, 2006:
http://www.gao.gov/archive/1996/ns96106.pdf.

————, *Acquisition Reform: DoD Faces Challenges in Reducing Oversight Costs,* report to congressional committees, Washington, D.C., GAO/NSIAD-97-48, January 1997a. As of May 3, 2006:
http://www.gao.gov/archive/1997/ns97048.pdf.

————, *Acquisition Reform: Effect on Weapon System Funding,* report to the Secretary of Defense, Washington, D.C., GAO/NSIAD-98-31, October 1997b. As of May 3, 2006:
http://www.gao.gov/archive/1998/ns98031.pdf.

Young, John, Assistant Secretary of the Navy for Research, Development, and Acquisition, memorandum for Deputy Secretary of Defense (Acting) and Under Secretary of Defense for Acquisition, Technology, and Logistics, Subject: Acquisition Document Process, July 22, 2005.